The Unstoppable
Church

The Unstoppable Church

A Pattern for the Future Church

David Shearman

New Wine Press

New Wine Ministries
PO Box 17
Chichester
West Sussex
United Kingdom
PO19 2AW

ISBN 978–1–905991–38–9

Typeset by CRB Associates, Reepham, Norfolk
Cover design by CCD, www.ccdgroup.co.uk
Printed in the United Kingdom

Dedication

Dedicated to the Glory of God

Contents

SECTION 4: The Unstoppable Church

Acknowledgements

To my family and friends, who though un-named, know that their love and friendship have always helped me.

To the companions I delight to work with and the wonderful congregation I am privileged to serve.

To J. John, for his incisive foreword and encouraging friendship.

To Tim Pettingale, whose tireless devotion and commitment have brought this book to completion.

To Charlotte Hall for her linguistic advice, to Mike Williams for his kind gift of the illustrations, to Andy Green for his energy and drive in the last weeks of preparation, and to Sarah Smellie, my daughter and secretary, for her enthusiastic help with the manuscript.

To my wife Dorothy Ann, who patiently helped me bring the project to life and keeps loving me.

And finally, to God for His unspeakable gift and endless love, thank You.

Preface

I am delighted that through the support of my good friend, Tim Pettingale, this new edition of *The Unstoppable Church* is in print. I still passionately believe the message developed in the early 1990s and published in 1996 and humbly contend that it is still as relevant as it ever was.

The Christian Church is seen as an institution alongside Parliament, Banks, Universities and so on. It is much more. It is an idea born in the heart of Almighty God and carries the "gilt edged" promise of its Founder, the Lord Jesus Christ, that He would build it and no power in the heavens or on earth would be able to stand against it. When all other institutions are finished and have faded away the Church will continue in eternity!

I have used the model of a medieval cathedral as a physical illustration of what the modern church should look like. It is used to help us see the bigger, more vibrant and dynamic reality of the Church as the Body of Christ, the hands and feet of Jesus in a tired and broken world.

The Church will be more effective in its mission of representing Jesus in every place in every generation, when . . .

1. It understands that it has been empowered and given authority.
2. It sees clearly its task and the power and effectiveness that comes from working together.

3. It takes seriously it's responsibility "to make disciples of all nations".

4. It holds to the conviction that no one and no thing can destroy it.

I invite you to explore these ideas in the pages that follow.

David Shearman
Nottingham, 2009

Foreword

Many have pleaded with Evangelicals to develop a sufficient ecclesiology for our times. An ecclesiology isn't an extension on a building or a trendy new theme of sociology or a way of welcoming people; it is, basically, a view of the Church. The accusation was that Evangelicals didn't have a full enough or significant enough view of the Church in order to maintain commitment in the next generation.

The growing Evangelical wing of the Church across the denominations needed to think about what it meant to be the people of God in a certain place. Have you ever wondered on a Sunday what on earth all this meeting together was really all about? If you've begun to wonder about the why? how? who? where? questions regarding the people of God, this book is a great place to start.

David Shearman takes us through what he perceives to be the essential elements in any church. Whether you perceive yourself to be in a position of leadership or not, this book will excite you with a vision of the Church. To those of you who are in positions of leadership in the Church, this book will provide both personally challenging material, as you continue to exercise the role to which God has called you, and also give clear and sound direction as you encourage and develop leaders and potential leaders around you.

I came across an interesting poem by William Dunbar called, *The Leader*:

I wanna be a leader.
I wanna be a leader.
Can I be a leader?
Can I? I can?
Promise? Promise?
Yippee, I'm a leader.
I'm a leader.
OK, what shall I do?

Some Christian churches I know in the United Kingdom and around the world seem to be in this position! So if you are a leader and you can't quite remember why or what you're a leader for, or even who you lead, then this book will be food and drink to you. If you are a leader and one of your congregation has bought you this, don't be offended; take it as a compliment that they think you're worth buying a book for!

I am an Anglican. So are many of the cathedrals in this country: Canterbury, Durham, York, St Paul's, etc. I have preached in a number of cathedrals over the years. And do you know, I don't know whether I really like them. Yet my friend, David Shearman, who is not an Anglican, but a Pentecostal, has re-envisioned the model of the original cathedral as a stunning image of what the Church in each city, town and village needs to be, in and of itself and for the wider community. Can you imagine that, in the same way in which, as you approach some towns, the most predominant image in the skyline is the House of God, if in reality the most predominant group in any city, town or village around were the people of God, a people built together as living stones to be a place where many could encounter God? That it was just impossible for someone to visit that place and not know there was a spiritual Cathedral of people? You will never be able to look at a cathedral again and not think about the things spoken of here.

Always practical, this book begins where many leave off, with the leaders, pleading for a thoroughly biblical and Spirit-filled perspective to leadership, challenging those in leadership positions in a new way. The Church is too important and its task is certainly too important to do in human strength, and time and again the initiative of God is stressed, in choosing the leaders, in building the vision, in giving the plan, in winning the victory. Then there are lessons for the whole Church, lessons from creation, the need to belong, the priority of prayer and the inspiration and confidence that God gives.

In his home town of Nottingham I have seen David Shearman work with God in doing just that. That's one of the reasons I can recommend this book so strongly to you. I have known David Shearman for approaching thirty years; he is a man who says what he means and means what he says. I have visited and preached on many occasions at the Christian Centre, the church he pastors. I have seen what he's done and read what he has said, and they match up. This isn't some new-fangled theory from the whizz-kids who have never been involved in the grass-roots Church. This is grass-roots stuff. Tried and tested, prayed and agonized over. I commend this book wholeheartedly.

If the vision of mighty living buildings or people in every place, living, moving, worshipping, proclaiming, learning, caring, forgiving, reaching out in the love and power of God, is biblical, then this is more than just good advice, or nice suggestions; it is the sum total of what the people of God are on earth to do and be.

Read on!

Canon J. John
The Philo Trust

Introduction

Some say that we live in a post-Christian era, concluding that the best days of the Christian religion are over. It is the epoch of reason; the mind, science and rationalism are among the new gods. Others are living in a "spiritual" world, variously focused in the drug culture often accompanied by music, in astrology with the Age of Aquarius mentality, or in one of the many streams of the polluted New Age river. Others are returning to the pagan spiritualities of our ancient cultures, while many more have no time for the mind gods or any spirituality, preferring to rush after the fanciful god of materialism with its many obsessions.

I am a Christian. I do not believe that I was born to live in a sinking ship called the Church. Jesus Christ is alive, the only God who became a man and the only man who permanently defeated death and the grave. He is the greatest person who has ever lived. He is my Saviour, a faithful friend of reliable pedigree who Himself said, *"I will build my Church, and the gates of hell will not overcome it."* Isaiah predicted that, *"Of the increase of His government and peace there will be no end."* This is what I believe. There is much evidence, especially around the developing world, that the Church is stronger now than at any time in its twenty centuries of existence, a fact which seems largely hidden from the European mind. It is for many an unknown, almost a secret. The Messiah who came to Bethlehem so long ago will come physically and visibly to earth again, I do not know when.

He will not come to a sinking ship, a lost cause, or for a tiny survivalist remnant, but rather for a radiant bride and a glorious Church which is without spot or blemish. This is *The Unstoppable Church* to which I belong and long to see bring great glory to God.

SECTION 1
Authority

The Cathedra

The Foundation of Authority

My wife Dorothy and I are still very much in love, after forty-three years of marriage. Dorothy enjoys reading whenever we take a few days' break; I prefer, among other things, to look at old buildings. During several of my visits to Britain's old cathedrals, I have asked myself many questions. Why did people build cathedrals? Why the setting and structure? What was their social, political and economic significance? If cathedrals were the greatest physical statement of medieval Christianity, what should their equivalent spiritual, and possibly physical, expression be in the so-called post-Christian era of the twenty-first century? Using the model of a medieval cathedral, throughout this book we will examine how modern Cathedrals of spiritual excellence – thousands of living stones joined together – may be built for the glory of God.

The word "cathedral" originates from the Latin word *cathedra* referring to the Bishop's chair which is housed there. This is the seat of authority and is a major key to the proper functioning of the whole structure. This seat, which is often rather ornate, has no power in itself, but it does, however, represent an authority. Who gives this authority? Who receives it? Who recognises it?

Tony Benn, a unique socialist MP of aristocratic birth is quoted,

"Whenever you meet a powerful person ask him these five questions:

1. What power have you got?
2. Where did you get it from?
3. In whose interests do you use it?
4. To whom are you accountable?
5. How do we get rid of you?"[1]

The Church, in its various expressions, claims authority for its leaders in a number of ways: apostolic succession; various forms of episcopacy; presbyterian rule by elders; congregational consensus; democracy; and, sadly, self-appointment. All manner of checks and balances are used to protect each structure, many with little or no biblical warrant. In the political arena, some parliaments work on various forms of *vox populi* – the voice and will of the people. Others are run by oligarchies, dictatorships, the gun, or a ruling family. There is huge variety. No system is perfect; many are tyrannical. But what does the Bible have to say about authority? In the Bible, the word "authority" is often accompanied by its companion, "power". *Exousia* is the original word for authority, with "right" or "privilege" as the simple translation. *Exousia* is also occasionally used for "power", but more often this is translated from the Greek word *dunamis*, meaning "ability" or "strength". For far-reaching, significant leadership to be established, authority and power must ride together.

Often when I'm preaching, I delight to adapt a simple story, depending on my whereabouts. This is the version I used recently during a visit to Guatemala:

The local water engineer arrives at Farmer Fernando's door armed with official papers, giving him authority to inspect the farmer's land because of problems with poisoned water. Fernando does not want the engineer on his land, but cannot refuse because proper authority has been given. While the engineer is changing his footwear, Fernando calls his son, Alphonso. "Go into the barn and untie Fidel," he whispers to the boy. "Let him loose in the big field." "Okay papa," replies Alphonso. Fernando continues smiling at the nameless water engineer, who goes off to his work. Through the gate and into the field, armed with his authority papers and other drawings, marches the unsuspecting government functionary. Fidel begins to show interest, then charges. The engineer waves his papers wildly, but Fidel the prize bull is not impressed. Old Fernando leans on the gate laughing, as, papers and all, the engineer beats a hasty retreat. The congregation laughs loudly. But, on a more serious note, how much does the Church parade its various institutional forms and papers signifying authority, and yet lack the power to deal with the forces ranged against it?

Immediately before His ascension, Jesus said to His disciples,

> *"All authority in heaven and on earth has been given to me. Therefore go and make disciples of all nations, baptising them in the name of the Father and of the Son and of the Holy Spirit."*
>
> (Matthew 28:18–19)

Until a proper, God-approved authority with power is in place, the Church drifts and lacks the direction and focus to complete its commission.

One sunny afternoon in Texas, I was spending some time with my friend Ron Corzine, an uninhibited enthusiast for Christ and one of the most spontaneous encouragers I have ever met. We were exchanging the revelations each of us had received from the Scriptures. Suddenly Ron said, "You must remember this. Preach it and remind people." "Go on," I said, "What is it?" There followed three statements:

1. The essence of life is Love (our **attitude**).
2. The issue of life is Law (our **authority**).
3. The spirit of life is Liberty (our **autonomy**).

I have thought about Ron's words many times and believe them more each time I think or speak about them. *The essence of life is love.* Love always hopes the best. Paul tells us that love is *"the most excellent way"* (1 Corinthians 12:31). *The spirit of life is liberty.* We are told that we have been set free for freedom (Galatians 5:1). But the focus of our present conversation is the second of the above statements: *the issue of life is law.* Every day, in every part of our life, the issue is law – authority. We stop for the policeman, work properly for our boss, leave other people's property alone, love our wife and help bring up our children. The politically correct movement doesn't want us to use some of this language. For instance, the phrase *"my wife"* conveys a sense of belonging, perhaps even ownership. (By the way, I am deliriously happy that Dorothy can say, "My husband, David" with the connotations already mentioned.) Why? Because the Bible says that in marriage two become one – they belong to each other. This is not restrictive but emancipating language. The strange philosophy of life being advocated by many modernists fails to address this "issue of life is law" argument, believing only in the law of what suits or pleases themselves. Maybe this is part of the decline eroding Western society.

I will say more about the Christian perspective and look at various levels of authority later. For now, we will concentrate on this seat of authority – the *cathedra* – for it seems to me that the dynamic possibilities of building the Cathedral with all its resources will fall short of its potential if the wrong person is sitting in the chair. Conversely, if the right "Bishop" sits in the *cathedra*, all the power and authority of New Testament Christianity is a possibility.

In John 1:6 we read,

"There came a man who was sent from God; his name was John."

It is this fundamental, almost irresistible calling of God, the fact of being set apart, anointed and commissioned, which is at the heart of leadership, ministry and service. Men and women are first appointed by God and are subsequently recognised by their fellows. In the days of Bible history, this type of person was identified, duly prepared and anointed for service. Christ's Church around the world, in all its denominational forms, needs a new bravery in our day to recognise those sent of the Lord. God-appointed and Holy Spirit anointed leaders are foundational in building today's spiritual cathedrals. Address this issue and the slow decline of Christian witness in Britain and Europe has the potential to turn into revival, joining forces with the dynamism of Christ's people in much of the developing world.

"You're a leader," some may retort. "You're simply devising a structure for an elite group, a cartel of cronies to operate in self-protection and promotion." Not at all, but I hope that this will become evident in the chapters that immediately follow. It is essential to have the right man in the right place doing the right thing at the right time. However, this alone will not translate into a Cathedral of living stones – a group of people who, together, make Jesus visible to the world. The leader needs a team: he must work in relationship with others gifted by God, but that is the second part of the book.

So far so good, but what else is required for Jesus to be seen in the life of the Church? It has been said,

> "The greatest waste in the world is the difference between what we are and what we could be."[2]

The greatest waste in the Church is the massive under-use of people's gifts and the under-development of their character. *"Go and make disciples,"* was the imperative word from Jesus before He physically left the world. Much of modern Christianity seems to have forgotten that injunction, preferring to tinker with church programmes, hide their true self and remain largely immature, unable to enjoy the full benefits of the inheritance open to them. Paul says that,

"As long as the heir is a child, he is no different from a slave."

(Galatians 4:1)

Elsewhere we read,

"In fact, though by this time you ought to be teachers, you need someone to teach you the elementary truths of God's word all over again."

(Hebrews 5:12)

It is vitally important that every individual is brought to maturity in Christ. This is one of our goals.

Are we beginning to get anywhere near the possibility of the Church being the fullness of Jesus, the expression of His life in a tired, bored world? I think so, and the consequences will be explosive, causing paradigm shifts in our thinking and operation. Imagine the drama of New Testament Christianity spilling out into the urban deprivation of inner cities and the comfortable boredom of the middle-classes, being reflected by dramatic changes in the figures that ooze out of statistics offices. These figures often represent hurting people, broken, disillusioned people, and you will find them in every social class, in every ethnic group. It is time that we allowed the Gospel, in all its power and glory, to touch our dying world with love. You will find my thoughts on these possibilities in the final chapters. I am a pilgrim myself. Please become a pilgrim with me and let us travel together through this book. It could just be to our mutual benefit.

Notes

1. Benn, T., MP, in a personal communication.
2. Herbster, B., *Life in Christ*, Issue 1. World Outreach, Hong Kong.

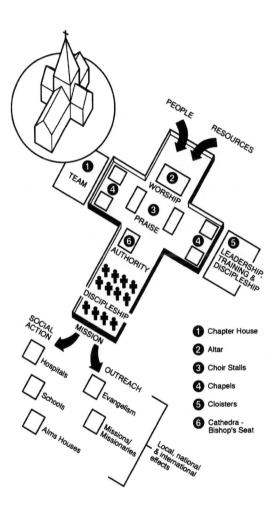

PEOPLE

RESOURCES

TEAM ①

② WORSHIP

④

③ PRAISE

⑥ AUTHORITY

④

⑤ LEADERSHIP, TRAINING & DISCIPLESHIP

DISCIPLESHIP

SOCIAL ACTION

MISSION

Hospitals

OUTREACH

Schools

Evangelism

Alms Houses

Missions/ Missionaries

Local, national & international effects

① Chapter House

② Altar

③ Choir Stalls

④ Chapels

⑤ Cloisters

⑥ Cathedra - Bishop's Seat

God-Anointed or Man-Appointed?

Paul paints big pictures in his Ephesian Epistle. Each individual Christian, after learning his position in Christ,[1] together with others, becomes "Church" (Ephesians 5:25). *"Christ loved the Church."* The Church is seen as a pure and lovely bride. Many a hard heart is moved by the sight of a beautiful virgin bride. Why is it, then, that in the developed world the Church has largely become so unattractive? Maybe the answer is simply that we have not maintained our love and devotion for the bridegroom, Jesus Christ, but have adulterated ourselves by loving others.

Paul has already presented two other gripping pictures: one is of a building. Unquestionably Christ Jesus is the chief cornerstone (Ephesians 2:20), but the fellow-citizens, God's people, are seen as members of God's household (Ephesians 2:19). This building includes the apostles and prophets as foundational. Are these people only the historic giants of our ancient faith, the "apostles of the lamb", and the seers of long ago, or may there be room for some twenty-first century applicants who are part of the footings of the present expression of the Church? This idea is very disconcerting for some; not only those whose dispensational theology makes no room for the present manifestation of Holy Spirit power, but, more alarmingly, for many Charismatics who have become so structured and democratic that such suggestions interfere with their religious cartels. But Paul's picture includes such God-appointed and Holy Spirit anointed persons as a necessity for the building. Every living stone is built and joined together to become a holy temple. Such a building becomes a dwelling in which God lives by His Spirit (Ephesians 2:22), which is a very different picture from the one presented by much of the Western Church today. Many Evangelical and Charismatic groups still have a back street, "small is beautiful" philosophy, and much main line Christianity is trapped with the problems of outdated and crumbling architecture – the "thermometer appeal for the new roof" syndrome – while the real Church, the people, are not being built together in a relevant, purposeful way.

As the beautiful bride of the picture is attractive, so this God-inspired building of living stones – human beings, touched by God's greatness, changed by grace and filled with glory – will attract a needy world to its sense of destiny and hope-filled Christianity.

We have looked at Paul's pictures in reverse order, but unlike the beauty pageant idea of third, second and first, each of the pictures is of equal importance. "The Church is His body," is Paul's emphatic statement (Ephesians 1:22–23). What do you think of when that picture is used? For me, many ideas spring readily to mind: the caring mother feeding a young child; the Olympic sprinter gracefully running to victory; the hard-working man. It is about beauty, coordination and usefulness. What has happened to Christ's Church? Is it as beautiful as it could be? Why does the Church look so uncoordinated and paralysed? Why does its leadership so often function with the grotesque independence of a one-man-band? Since the Church in the West spends in excess of ninety percent of its resources on itself, how useful is it in fulfilling its task of taking the Good News of Jesus to every people group? But the Church is His body. Paul says it is to be,

" . . . *the fullness of Him who fills everything in every way.*"

(Ephesians 1:23)

One key seems to be in how the body is joined to Christ who has been appointed "Head" over everything. This is a statement of authority. I have already expressed that the issue of life is always law, or authority. The verses immediately preceding Paul's statement strongly declare that Christ, in being raised from the dead, has been exalted to a position above all rule and authority, power and dominion, above every title that can be given, for now, and in the future; and that's the top job! Head of the table! Leader of the pack! In Bible language,

> "KING OF KINGS AND LORD OF LORDS."   (Revelation 19:16)

Paul insists that the Church, the body of Christ, is to be the fullness of Him, which must mean that He has given us a right, a name and the authority to act at this time. However, most of the Church, as I have observed in my many travels around the world, seems to fall far short of this high calling. But does this mean that we should not speak of what the Bible says is God's purpose for His Church? Of course not. What does this authority language mean? Turn back the pages of Bible history with me. I will briefly examine five authority models and then relate them to the Church today.

1. Adam's Rule in Creation

In the staggering description of creation, God gives to Adam a specific privilege, several blessings and clear responsibility. It is sad that many in our modern world have separated these things. Privilege and blessing don't work well without the balance of responsibility. Adam's privileges included headship over creation and being created in God's image and likeness. He was blessed,

emotionally –

> "It is not good for the man to be alone. I will make a helper suitable for him."   (Genesis 2:18)

socially –

> *"The Lord God took the man and put him in the Garden of Eden to work it and take care of it."*   (Genesis 2:15)

morally –

> *"You are free to eat from any tree in the garden; but you must not eat from the tree of the knowledge of good and evil."*
>
> (Genesis 2:16–17)

and **spiritually** – the implication is strong that God was coming to have fellowship with Adam and Eve when they were hiding from Him after the fall (Genesis 3:9). God had spent time communicating with His creation as the statements above exemplify.

Has it ever occurred to you that on the seventh day, according to the Genesis account, when Adam woke to his first sunrise, all the aforementioned privileges and blessings were already his; he had not worked for or earned them? Maybe he asked God about the possibility of doing something to help creation along? God could have replied, "Take a day off, Adam, I have finished everything!" So Adam's first full day on earth was a day of rest. In other words, he worked after rest rather than resting after work. Why don't Christian leaders learn this lesson? As Hebrews 4 teaches us, *"There is a rest for the people of God."* Why doesn't all humanity understand that when Jesus Christ cried out on the cross, *"It is finished,"* He had redeemed and bought back all the privileges and blessings that Adam forfeited? We cannot attain them by trying hard to be a Christian, doing good, praying fervently or anything else. We must realise that all our salvation, every blessing, is through grace because of what Jesus accomplished. Once we have entered this rest we shall work hard, but for a different reason.

Adam had privileges, blessings and also responsibilities, which included a command to be fruitful and increase in number, and to rule over every living creature (Genesis 1:28). It is not my

purpose to argue any ecological viewpoint in this book, although
the issue is very germane. I prefer to make the simple but
profound point that the God of creation delegated a responsible
and demonstrable authority to the one created in His image,
Adam.

2. Abraham's Blessing for the Nations

The pages of Genesis turn and we glimpse many secrets
about God's character and ways. For example, He deals with
sin only through blood sacrifice; an unpleasant but necessary
fact (inferred by Genesis 3:21). In chapter 11 He deals
with man's oft-repeated scheme to *"make a name for ourselves"*
(verse 4) in the showdown at the tower of Babel. Man's self-
help schemes and name-making are legendary through the
centuries. The chapter ends with a pagan called Abram. God
decides to make his name great, unleashing an array of "I will's"
that are to make a significant impact on Abram, his family and
the world.

> *"I will make you into a great nation and I will bless you; I will*
> *make your name great, and you will be a blessing. I will bless*
> *those who bless you, and whoever curses you I will curse; and*
> *all people on earth will be blessed through you."*
>
> (Genesis 12:2–3)

Personal, territorial, national and spiritual blessings are among
the list of staggering benefits. God says, *"All peoples on earth will*
be blessed through you" (Genesis 12:3). This is a powerful authority statement; the God of eternity makes an apparently arbitrary
choice – Abram – and declares that all ethnic groups on earth
will be blessed through him. In the same way that Adam could
not have assumed his role of rule, neither could Abram have
decided such a fate. Both of them were delegated the authority
to function in a specific way.

3. A Priest Between God and the People

In the exodus from Egypt, Aaron, the chosen High Priest, is spoken of as entering God's presence wearing the names of the different tribes of Israel on his clothes (Exodus 28:29). There are many other pictures, all leading to the same conclusion: one man was allowed to represent a larger group in its relationship with God. A true understanding of the powerful nature of an Almighty, Omnipotent God leads us to conclude that permission must have been granted for anyone to approach Him either on his own or someone else's account. Again we have an authority statement: God says that in certain circumstances one human being can represent others before God to good effect and no personal harm (see Leviticus 10).

4. A King to Lead the People

Israel's first king, Saul, is anointed with oil (1 Samuel 10). The prophet Samuel said to him, *"Has not the LORD anointed you leader over His inheritance?"* Without labouring the point, it is clear that a position of leadership – that is, one man making decisions that impact the lives of others – requires the permission of a higher authority. God gave this authority: *"Listen to them and give them a king"* (1 Samuel 8:22). So authority may be delegated by God to a person to lead others on God's behalf.

5. A Prophet to Speak to the People

God makes an amazing statement when He says to Jeremiah, *"Now, I have put my words in your mouth"* (Jeremiah 1:9) and continues, *"I appoint you over nations and kingdoms."* This is strong language. God's words, thoughts and ideas are relayed through the mind and mouth of a chosen person. This is a big responsibility and a serious delegation of God's authority.

In summary, what do these five authority models show us?

1. Man can rule in specific areas of life.
2. Man can be a blessing to others.
3. Man can take a position as intercessor.
4. Man can lead others.
5. Man can speak to others on God's behalf.

Striding the pages of history, which single individual embodies all these characteristics? Whilst respecting those who follow other religions, it isn't a Buddha or a Mohammed, or any other prophet or god. The position requires the applicant to have demonstrated clear qualifications in each area.

Jesus Christ is the only Credible Candidate!

1. In which specific areas did He rule?
He walked on water, turned water into wine, opened the eyes of the blind, raised the dead, stilled the storm and much more. He is identified as the son of Adam (Luke 3:38), the last Adam (1 Corinthians 15:45; not the "second", as is so often misquoted). Why the last? Because He so utterly succeeded that there will be no more. His authority is certainly demonstrated in His rule over the created order.

2. Which people, race or nationality did He bless?
The genealogy in Matthew's gospel does not concentrate on establishing Christ's link with Adam, preferring to start at Abraham (Matthew 1:1–17). Thus, via David, Abraham's blessings from Genesis 12:1–3 become Christ's. Did the authority to bless other people groups pass with dignity to Jesus? He cut across Jewish custom to help the Samaritan woman at Sychar's well (John 4). While taking a short holiday, He set a young foreigner free from demonic power at Caesarea Philippi (Mark 9:14–29). The Roman soldier, himself *"a man under authority"*

to quote his revealing words, pleaded successfully for the Christ to, *"Just say the word, and my servant will be healed"* (Matthew 8:4–13). Before the remarkable events of the cross, tomb and resurrection, which offer a blessing to every person in every people group on earth, the Lord Jesus had clearly demonstrated His authority to bless those outside His family group. After the cross we can only conclude that this son of Abraham fulfils to the letter the Genesis 12 prophecy. He clearly has the authority to bless all people.

3. For whom did He act as high priest and intercessor?
There are many verses in Hebrews which identify Jesus as a priest. Hebrews 4:14 extols Him as *"A great high priest."* Chapter 7 states that He was not an Aaronic Levitical priest, but followed the more mystical order of Melchizedek, the priest-king of Salem (Genesis 14:18). The weight of the New Testament teaching reveals Jesus as the ultimate priest and the absolute sacrifice. He offers up His own life as a payment for all sin and now lives and reigns forever and sends His Spirit to make the benefits of His extraordinary accomplishments available to ordinary people who call on His name for grace and mercy. Without doubt, Jesus, both fully God and fully man, has the authority to stand between God and mankind in intercession.

4. What about Jesus' authority as a leader?
I will choose only to quote His reply under Pilate's questioning: *"You are right in saying I am a king. In fact, for this reason I was born"* (John 18:37). His lineage is undisputed: He is a son of David (Mark 1:6; Luke 3:31). Through the open door in heaven we see, *"A white horse, whose rider is called Faithful and True"* (Revelation 19:11), who is also named, *"KING OF KINGS AND LORD OF LORDS"* (Revelation 19:16). That which so many people call the Lord's prayer (*"Your Kingdom come, your will be done"*) will find its ultimate fulfilment when Christ is recognised as King of all.

He has an undisputed pedigree. Jesus the Anointed One is chosen to lead as King.

5. Did Jesus have the ability to speak to others on God's behalf? His prophetic claims are remarkable by any definition of a prophet. Whether foretelling, forthtelling, or receiving knowledge through revelation, He qualifies. Some say prophets should be known by their intimacy with God, intercession, inspiration and insight. Jesus the prophet scored full marks, ten out of ten. Some were heard to say about Him, *"No one ever spoke the way this man does"* (John 7:46); another claimed that He, *"Told me everything I ever did"* (John 4:29). He said Himself, *"Whatever I say is just what the Father has told me to say"* (John 12:50). He had the authority to speak as the mouthpiece of God. A prophet indeed.

Where does all this lead us? If the Church is to be the fullness of Him who fills everything in every way, having first established that Jesus Christ's claim to have all power and authority is legitimate and justified, we must conclude that His body should demonstrate a rule in the created world, an ability to bless all the families on earth, a power in prayer and intercession, an authority to lead in God's name, and an anointing to speak as His mouthpiece. What a privilege! What a challenge! Thank God for every miracle, every missions enterprise, every prayer, every example, and every inspired word; but how much more is available, delegated by the Head of the Church! The release of this power and authority means that we can be His fullness to a needy, lost and fear-filled world. That is the Cathedral of living stones, the living body and this beautiful bride that I want to belong to. Then the world will see a true picture of Jesus, not some tired caricature trapped in religion, nor entombed in buildings, but the fullness of Him who fills everything in every way.

Before leaving the pictures of Ephesians, I invite you to meditate on the following truths with me. Abiding in them will change us. We will be able to live more effectively as part of Christ's Church, expressing His fullness through our lives.

1. I am special to God. I am blessed and adopted (Ephesians 1:3).
2. I am chosen by God (Ephesians 1:4).
3. I am included and marked in Christ (Ephesians 1:13–14).
4. I am created for good works (Ephesians 2:10).
5. I am alive with Christ (Ephesians 2:5).

Notes

1. For an excellent exposition on this matter read Watchman Nee, *Sit, Walk, Stand,* available from various publishers.

Politics or the Hand of God?

When the authority that Jesus Christ has invested in His Church (and, more specifically, the clear authority delegated through leadership) is truly realised, it is necessary for us to find appropriate methods of recognising our leaders at every level.

I think back to a time when I was teaching at an overseas pastors' conference . . .

As well as the inspirational dimension, the delegates are conducting necessary denominational business, including the selection of a new national leader. Among the five hundred or more leaders, one or two are easily recognised (by several of us) as gifted men with maturity, anointing and proven fruit from their years of ministry. Why are they not further recognised? "Because we have always used a democratic system," I think the answer would be. Consequently, the conference is presented with thirteen names.

This scenario could be repeated worldwide. Due to the democratic system, the list of candidates can frequently include a combination of democrats, caring pastors, evangelists, egocentric power-seekers, devoted men with great hearts who are willing to serve but who possess little anointing to lead, politicians, administrators, and finally some anointed leaders. The list can be added to or subtracted from at will.

Returning to my pastors' conference: the group elects a polit-
ician whose acceptance speech is more reminiscent of J.F.
Kennedy than any biblically-based call to advance the Kingdom
of God. The outcome of such a situation is generally that the
anointed men go back to their own successful work, multiply
churches, inspire a new generation of leaders immediately
around them, and see thousands of people meeting together in
the name of Jesus. But what of the remainder? The result of
stagnation and infighting, coupled with a loss of vision and
direction, is that a new generation is not raised up in the power
of the Spirit and the work does not therefore advance as it could
and should have done. The principles manifested in the illustration given occur wherever this Spirit-stifling democracy has
prevalence.

What alternative picture could be painted in place of the
illustration above? Senior leaders, after prayer, could have agreed
upon the most gifted, anointed and appropriate leader, and
offered his name to the rest of the conference for their affirmation. God has *one person*, be it a Moses, a Joseph or a David,
prepared for a particular task. Why insult Him by offering
thirteen possibilities?

A wise, humble, anointed leader would then gather others
– including the pastors who care and the administrators who
have gifts to organise and steer – and together with them, as a
team, work in such a way that what happened locally would
have an impact on millions of people in the whole region. This
would work better than the present democratic system, locally,
regionally or nationally. It is highly probable that the recognition
of biblically qualified elders in the local churches, working with
Ephesians 4:11 ministries, would provide an even better model
of leadership in the Church, which would be closer to the
model illustrated by the New Testament Church.

My vote goes to the system that recognises the leaders whom
God has already chosen, refined and anointed. Let's stop our
appointing and simply affirm, recognise or agree upon those

whom the Head of the Church has already called and appointed. As a direct result, every denomination or doctrinal grouping would be more reliant on the Lord and more attentive to the voice of the Spirit, and therefore unavoidably more successful.

But from this hypothesis a question arises which first requires answering:

"How can we recognise these anointed, God-appointed leaders?"

God's Selection Criteria

Through the millennia God has chosen people for His service. It may be a pagan called Abram (Genesis 12:1); a teenage boy – Joseph (Genesis 37:5); an educated runaway – Moses (Exodus 2:11); the least of the least – Gideon (Judges 6:11); a man head and shoulders above the rest – Saul (1 Samuel 9:1); or the young, ruddy-faced sheep farmer – David (1 Samuel 16:12).

Taking the illustration of the "choosings" of Saul and David, one first recognises the role of Samuel the prophet. Samuel was authorised by God to go and commission Saul for the kingship in response to the people's desire to have a king to lead them, *"Such as the other nations have"* (1 Samuel 8:5), but only after he had given them a strong prophetic warning that they were missing God's best.

There are lessons to learn from the anointing of Saul which have contemporary relevance (1 Samuel 10). A young man is concerned over the loss of his father's donkeys, but Samuel says to him, *"The donkeys you set out to look for have already been found"* (verse 2). So firstly, the anointing helps to solve yesterday's problems. Then the prophet promises Saul that he will meet three men who will offer him loaves of bread which he will accept (verse 4). Secondly then, the anointing is important in the meeting of today's needs. Samuel closes by saying that the new king will meet a procession of prophets, that the Spirit of the Lord will be upon him and that he will prophesy and be changed (verses 5–6). Thirdly, we see that the anointing provides the word of the Lord for future direction. Samuel sadly watched Saul's life move from this fresh anointing and dependence on God through phases of disobedience to the rejection we find in chapter 16. Saul next comes to the fore as the leading player in the opening scenes of David's story. The Lord challenges him to stop mourning over past failure because, in paraphrase, "I've chosen someone else" (1 Samuel 16:1).

Before we look at the impact of this anointing on the life of David, what keys does the Bible hold about this anointing with oil? It must be seen metaphorically as the coming of the Spirit.

Psalm 23:5 says, *"You anoint my head with oil,"* speaking the language of welcome to an honoured guest invited to a family meal. Oil is often used, particularly with regard to the Old Testament priesthood, to demonstrate separateness, a belonging to God and separation from the normal affairs of this world (see for example Exodus 30:29).

Isaiah teaches us that the anointing breaks the yoke (Isaiah 10:27 KJV). John says that we have an anointing from the Holy One (1 John 2:20), and then affirms that the anointing we have received remains in us (1 John 2:27). Psalm 78:70–72 says,

> *"He* [the Lord] *chose David His servant*
> *and took him from the sheep pens;*
> *from tending the sheep He brought him*
> *to be shepherd of His people Jacob,*
> *of Israel His inheritance.*
> *And David shepherded them with integrity of heart;*
> *with skilful hands he led them."*

Psalm 89:20 underlines this choosing by God, saying,

> *"I have found David my servant;*
> *with my sacred oil I have anointed him."*

What can we learn from the ancient history of David in order to release a great outflow of God's anointing and authority through us to meet our world's needs? Life is a pilgrimage, a journey and a development, and for David there were to be three distinct and progressive anointings. First in Bethlehem in the context of his family, Samuel was instructed to anoint this young teenager, even though naturally his brothers appeared to be better suited to the task in hand. With this anointing came a new sense of direction, as well as determination, wisdom and power from God. Some years later the tribal group, Judah, recognised God's calling on David (2 Samuel 2:4) and gathered together to anoint him king over their house. This is a wider anointing, a tribal, regional recognition of God's hand on the young man's life. Then in 2 Samuel 5:3 all the elders of Israel came to recognise him as king. This was more than a local, family anointing or a tribal, regional anointing; it was a recognition that he was king over the nation.

Has anything changed? Do we expect people to succeed on the national or international scene who have never proved the calling of God in their own region or locality, or have not shown evidence of God's anointing in the everyday affairs of life? The example of David is a pattern for the development of God's anointing in every generation.

This overview of David's developing anointing is simplistic and does not elaborate on the way in which the faithfulness of God shapes and develops him as a leader through the landmarks of his life, but it serves as a framework for further observation and understanding. Others have taught the following principles, but they bear repetition and serve to show how we are to recognise God's anointed.

What is happening to David at Bethlehem, as he works for his father at home? He is doing what he is told, carrying the sandwiches to the war front, looking after the sheep, and killing the lion and the bear when no-one is watching (1 Samuel 17). In other words, he is being *faithful in natural things*. No one will succeed as an anointed servant of God without first being faithful in the natural affairs of life. This means being obedient in our work situations with honesty and enthusiasm, overcoming our personal weaknesses and the pressures of our circumstances, and flourishing in the everyday relationships of family: this is being faithful in natural things.

Later on we find David in Adullam's Cave (1 Samuel 22). The desperadoes, the debtors, deserters and general flotsam and jetsam of life make up his new surroundings. He trains and disciplines these men until they become a worthy fighting force, an honourable band of loyal, devoted men. David proves himself to be *faithful in need*.

Then the Amalekites raid Ziklag (1 Samuel 30). What despair overtook them! Their wives and families are kidnapped while they are fighting God's cause. His men are bitter in spirit and David himself is greatly distressed, but he encourages himself in the Lord and strengthens the resolve of his brothers. They regain their lost families and treasure, and reward their enemies dutifully. David has proved himself *faithful in trouble*. So many people panic, losing their confidence in difficult situations, but the anointed remain faithful. Remember, it is written,

> *"If you falter in times of trouble,*
> *how small is your strength!"*   (Proverbs 24:10)

Then to Hebron, geographically the highest place on the journey, where David develops relationships with his tribal brothers (2 Samuel 2) – one of the hardest, most painful experiences of life, but thankfully also one of its most rewarding joys. All anointed men will prove themselves *faithful in relationships*. I will write later about the joy and pain of developing a team and living in relationship.

And finally to Zion, the place of rule. He sends his soldiers to dispossess the Jebusites from their stronghold. The Jebusites had resisted the advance of Israel into the promised land for over four hundred years, but now God's anointed leader is issuing the orders and his soldiers capture the fortress. David is welcomed into the place of rule and proves himself to be both a man of mercy and integrity when he has the power to deal harshly with people. He is *faithful in rule*. Immediately after this the Philistines attack him at the place of giants, the valley of Rephaim. However, David calls it Baal Perazim, the place where God breaks through (2 Samuel 5:20).

So David has proved himself through the journey of his life to be faithful in natural things, faithful in need, faithful in trouble, faithful in relationships and faithful in rule. The generations have passed but the principles remain. Here is a key to recognising anointed leadership: *all who are anointed of God will have passed the same landmarks and will have proven the same principles in the daily practice of their life.*

One Sunday morning, during a fairly ordinary service, the Lord challenged me to prophesy around the theme in 1 Chronicles 11 of Benaiah, who destroyed a lion in a pit on a snowy day. I obeyed and the service broke through into something new. The Spirit of God spoke to me again from the passage later that same evening. What He said to me can be applied to our present conversation. The scripture says that this anointed, experienced man, Benaiah, dealt with three distinct enemies: two Moabites, a lion in a pit and a tall Egyptian.

In the Bible, the people of Moab were those who tried to stop the children of Israel reaching their promised land, their future and their possibilities (Numbers 22–25). All anointed people must learn to remove and overcome everything that seeks to limit their future. "I'm not good enough . . . not trained enough . . . I don't speak well . . . I'm afraid I might fail . . . Has God really promised me . . . ?" That kind of thinking and speaking will *restrict your future*. Rise up and destroy your "Moabites"!

Then Benaiah finds himself in a pit with a lion on a snowy day. Lions do not usually leave a pit. That means it's him or you. If you don't kill your spiritual enemies they will kill you. These conflicts rarely take place on the days when you feel good, full of life and confidence in God. No! They come on cold, hard, snowy days when you'd prefer to sit by the fire and take a little nap. You may feel uncertain and be lacking in spiritual zeal, but you must rise up and fight, for the things that seek to *rob your present* will not leave uninvited. Destroy that lion!

Finally, Benaiah faces an Egyptian man, seven-and-a-half feet tall. Benaiah has removed the opposition that tried to restrict his future and rob his present. Now he comes across an enemy that *reminds him of the past*. The Bible portrays Egypt as a place of past slavery, limitation and bondage. Yesterday's failure, insecurity, hereditary limitations, past rejection, "Who am I anyway?" feelings; they must all be dealt the death blow. If you don't gain the victory here, then your effectiveness will be greatly limited. Thank God that in Christ we have the power! He has triumphed over every opposition that would attempt to drag us back to our yesterdays, rob our todays and limit our tomorrows.

The biblical illustrations are numerous: Joseph, Moses, David, Benaiah, to say nothing of the years of preparation prior to the public ministry of our Saviour Jesus, or the wilderness that was the Apostle Paul's journey – all to bring God's servants to the place of effective, anointed ministry. The outcome of such people is history, very dramatic history. What will be written about you and me?

Do it God's Way

A line from one of the favourite songs of the twentieth century, "I did it my way," is more than words to a tune. It portrays a whole philosophy of life venerated by modern man: "If it suits me it's okay . . . if I like it, then the consequences for others don't matter . . . if it feels good, do it."

A pluralistic, multi-faith, or hedonistic and selfish approach to life will allow room for undefined views about many things, including God, life, death and authority. The Christian view, however, is much more defined. God is the creator of all and the absolute authority in the Universe. Life given by Him is therefore sacred and death is not negotiable from any human perspective. In the words of Job,

> *"The LORD gave and the LORD has taken away;*
> *may the name of the LORD be praised."* (Job 1:21)

Any departure from this somewhat rigid standpoint leaves us in a moral, medical and emotional maze as man reinvents himself as a god. An attempt to define a Christian view of authority reveals four distinct areas, beginning, as stated above, with the absolute and total authority of God Almighty. He is before all things and is not required to agree or negotiate with any person or power. He makes His own rules and laws according to His will and pleasure. If the God of the Bible were the fearsome, demanding, insatiable beast of some of the world's religions, then to describe Him as a despot would indeed be a restrained definition. But God is not like that. Sure, there are many things that are hard to understand: suffering, unfairness, apparent injustice; but God is good. He has the welfare of His creation, especially man, as His highest priority and has provided a framework for life which, when followed, brings endless blessing and benefit to the individual, the family and society. To coin a phrase, "He rules, OK". The *first level of authority* is stated thus: He has sovereign authority. If He says, "Jump!" the question is, "How high?" not, "Why?"

The opening salvos of the Bible in Genesis 1 reveal, among other things, that God is a communicator. *"Let there be light"* (verse 3), He says to an apparently formless and empty earth. Then He speaks to Himself within the Trinity, saying, *"Let us make man in our image"* (verse 26; If God talks to Himself it cannot be a sign of madness after all. What a relief!) God then speaks to the man and woman, *"Be fruitful and increase in number"* (verse 28), giving instructions, promises and responsibility.

The awful events of the fall then follow, unfolding shadows of pain and separation that reach the very heart of God at the cross of Jesus. Adam embarks upon man's oft-repeated blame shifting routine,

> *"The woman you put here with me – she gave me some fruit from the tree, and I ate it."*   (Genesis 3:12)

A short conversation follows in which God speaks specifically and very directly to the talking serpent, to the woman (as yet apparently unnamed), and to Adam. God is therefore able to communicate at different levels: with Himself, with man and woman, with His wider creation and, if we accept the serpent as a personification of Lucifer, with Satan and the angelic kingdom.

The Bible expresses that God has honoured His name and His word above all things (Psalm 138:2). Speaking of itself, the Bible says that,

> *"All scripture is God-breathed and is useful . . . "*
>
> (2 Timothy 3:16)

Many scholarly words have been written amplifying the point that the Bible is not just another "holy book" or a collection of historical records, but a unique and specific manifestation of God, speaking to all of the groups previously identified. The evangelical Christian view is that the Bible is God's Word. The Westminster Confession states,

> The whole counsel of God concerning all things necessary for His own glory, man's salvation, faith and life, is either expressly set down in Scripture, or by good and necessary consequence may be deduced from Scripture: Unto which nothing at any time is to be added, whether by new revelations of the Spirit, or traditions of men.[1]

Our approach to God, our lives, ourselves and all other relationships must be based on its teaching. Under God's absolute authority, His Word – the Bible – is the *second level of authority*.

"Made in God's image" is the divine testimony of all humans. We have not come "from the goo, through the zoo, to you," as some would have it. A God-given conscience is part of our unique position in creation. The Bible speaks of us having a good conscience (1 Timothy 1:5; 1 Peter 3:21) and warns against following the hypocritical teaching of people with seared consciences which are damaged beyond normal function (1 Timothy 4:2). Incidentally, have you noticed that even very young children show signs of a conscience at work regardless of any parental discipline? The conscience is God's *third level of authority*, disobeyed at personal cost and societal pain.

Accepting that the law of conscience will never disobey the law of Scripture, which will in turn never contradict the nature and character of God, leads us to the tangible outworking of God's authority in human society – the *fourth level of authority* – authority which has been delegated by God. This is expressed in many distinct forms, including governmental responsibility, parental responsibility, and within church leadership to name but three. I have been involved in the latter at most levels for almost fifty years. Such a period has given me ample opportunity to observe that "pull" works better than "push". In other words, grace works better than law. In a strange mixture, the Church of Jesus is both a divine organism and a voluntary organisation: you belong by supernatural happening – new birth – but you function by free will and choosing to be available.

So how does the delegated authority of anointed Christian leadership work best? The Sergeant Major, barking out orders? The democracy, when only the will of the majority is allowed? Or by some unguided, "everyone obeys the Spirit" free for all? I have found some principles in Psalm 110 that have helped me lead the people of God. The psalm opens with the Almighty affirming the position of His Son,

> *"The Lord says to my Lord:*
> *'Sit at my right hand*
> *until I make your enemies*
> *a footstool for your feet.'"*

Christ's own statement . . .

> *"All authority in heaven and on earth has been given to me"*
> (Matthew 28:18)

. . . is the outworking of the prophetic observation of the psalm. The Church, and society in all its factions, works better when God-approved, God-anointed and God-appointed leaders maintain godly order under Christ's headship and authority. Opposition to God's will and the interference of spiritual enemies is neutralised (Psalm 110:2) and God's people are co-operative and willing. In a community where willingness and voluntary support are vital, this divine atmosphere of preparation – *"Your troops will be willing"* (Psalm 110:3) – is essential.

The balance of the psalm now changes, concentrating not only on the authority and power dimension of rule, but also the compassion, intercession and interest of a priest. Verse four prophetically identifies Jesus with that strange, *"order of Melchizedek"* priesthood, and Hebrews 7:17 echoes the psalm, *"You are a priest for ever in the order of Melchizedek."* The writer of Hebrews has already established that Jesus is a great high priest:

> *"Therefore, since we have a great high priest who has gone through the heavens, Jesus the Son of God, let us hold firmly to the faith we profess. For we do not have a high priest who is unable to sympathise with our weaknesses, but we have one who has been tempted in every way, just as we are – yet was without sin. Let us then approach the throne of grace with confidence, so that we may receive mercy and find grace to help us in our time of need."*
>
> (Hebrews 4:14–16)

Jesus understands how we feel. He has stood where we stand. Leaders must have this interest for and empathy with the people who are under their care. Jesus loves and cares for us; people need to be sure that their leaders love and care for them. Jesus prays and makes intercession for us; our people will instinctively know whether or not we pray for them. These principles will make strong and decisive leaders, themselves submitted to higher authority, filled with love, care and compassion. The leaders will then enjoy the blessing of "willing troops" in the church, the home, the workplace and in business. I believe that Church denominations and national governments would function much better if more attention were paid to applying the godly principles of Psalm 110.

Due to a powerful view of Christianity expressed in service, suffering and dying to self, many of my conservative Evangelical and Catholic readers may have found the preceding chapters on authority difficult to embrace. I do not doubt for one moment that if *"I bear on my body the marks of Jesus"* (Galatians 6:17), then the glory of His resurrection life will radiate through me. But as in so many other issues, these apparent opposites – Christ expressed in selfless service and Christ expressed in delegated authority – must be embraced with equal priority by all the branches of Christ's Church. I am delighted that having expressed myself on the issue of authority, I will presently address the issue of the selfless service of Christ's Body, the Church, and the inevitable maturing of the "Cathedral".

We have spent enough time sitting in and walking around the *cathedra*, the bishop's chair, the seat of authority. Let me re-emphasise some of the high ground already stated: every day, the issue of life is law. God's ultimate rule and authority are awesome, and grasping even a limited understanding of the areas He has delegated, and the people whom He has designated, brings a breathtaking dynamism to the leadership of Christ's body, the Church, and the potential to reach the elements of life and society that nothing else can touch.

As you drive into the City of York from the south, before the city itself comes into view, the huge mass of the ancient cathedral, York Minster, dominates the skyline. Would to God the living stones of His Church in every community were as noticeable, being effective as His light and salt, so that the fabric of society could function as God intended because the Cathedral of living stones was in place. The Church will only work correctly when the authority issue is understood and the right leadership is in place. Important though that chair may be, there is more to a cathedral – much more. Walk with me through the choir stalls and turn into the Chapter House, the arena in which senior leaders work together, where we will explore the next part of this vision.

Notes

1. *The Westminster Confession of Faith.* Quoted by Wayne Grudem, *Systematic Theology,* IVP, Leicester, 1994, p. 1180.

SECTION 2
Team

The Chapter House

Do You See
What I See?

My friend John Shelbourne, who sadly is no longer with us, delighted to paraphrase Isaiah 60:5 from the Authorised Version, "Those that see together flow together." A clear vision and stated goals are obviously part of this "seeing-together" process. For people to "flow together" it is essential for them to understand the construction, purpose and motivation of *team*. This will enable them to build the church and develop the body so that it is effective and useful. In this context, let us define *team* as a set number of people who are working towards a specific goal within given parameters.

It is my reflection that too few teams exist in a form that will enable the Body of Christ to come to maturity. There are still far too many one-man-band leadership models, which often reproduce themselves. Most frequently the leader will be a pastor (regarding his gifts and abilities) and at first sight is a hard working, devoted and godly individual. Closer acquaintance often reveals a kindly but insecure personality which finds it difficult to delegate, slow to train and disciple other leaders, ineffective in recognising potential leadership, and very often loath to receive helpful constructive observation from others.

Some leaders, recognising the paralysing limitations of a non-team ministry, have tried to solve the problem by involving people in many areas of ministry, misguidedly thinking that they're building a team. However, the basic building blocks required for *team* are not in place and all that develops is a mishmash of well-intentioned enthusiasts or a series of glorified rotas.

Imagine a group of leaders working together – it's not *team*, but they're all busy. They think that working together means that each should have his turn to preach in the main services. One of the group is of a gentle pastoral nature, another is a good evangelist and a third is one of those "deep" Bible teachers. Next Sunday morning it is the turn of the teacher. A newly converted family are bringing their children to be blessed. They are outgoing people, have many friends and are going to use this opportunity to bring their friends to church. Is the "deep" teacher really the best person for the job? No, but it's his turn. This is not an example of a dynamic, interactive team!

In my youth I enjoyed various sports, not least playing wing three-quarter in rugby union and as a goalkeeper in soccer. In both of these positions one can spend long periods without being vitally involved in the game, but when great agility and bravery is required to score a try or to save a goal, one needs the right person doing the right thing in the right place at the right time. To further emphasise the point, imagine a building site. Fred is a hard-working conscientious bricklayer. He is good at his job, fast and reliable. Don't make the mistake of assuming that because he can build walls efficiently wherever he is told to, however, that he is capable of running the whole multimillion dollar project. This calls for Charlie the architect, who has little idea how to build a wall, but can manage a site efficiently.

In other words, we need apostolically gifted people (Ephesians 4:11) who know how to "read the plans". These are prophetic people who can see what needs to happen in the future and leaders who can build the right mixture of gifts together into *team*. What is *team*? What do I see? Use the sport or building metaphor to help you focus. *Team* must have a defined membership; it must have a clear purpose and work for a specified time.

What is the point of having eleven goal keepers in a soccer team? You need to achieve a balance of gifts and abilities. The major soccer clubs may have many players available in a first team pool, but only a defined number are named on the team sheet for each match. Their purpose is clear to them: "Win the match by scoring more goals than the opposition – and it must all happen in ninety minutes."

The building site metaphor has a wider application. The senior group who run the project know what they are building and the timescale that the customer has demanded. Within the overall project there are many sub-contractors, specific groups who also know who is in their team, what they are doing and how long they have to complete the task. This illustration is very helpful in understanding the building of Church. After all, we are that *"Building which is joined together and rises to become a holy temple in the Lord"* (Ephesians 2:21). As such we are part of an overall plan designed by God in eternity. No wonder the whole of creation is "on tip-toes waiting in eager expectation" (Romans 8:19, J.B. Phillips).

A strong thriving local church will involve within the leadership team many specific groups of people, each with their own clear purpose and personnel. They are all working together on the project, which is seeing the Church become what the architect and chief builder, Jesus Christ, designed it to be. The stronger the church is, the more diverse the areas of ministry served by its many teams will be. All must be accountable to one another and work towards the overall vision.

In our Cathedral model, the Bishop, who for us is the anointed, God-appointed and man-affirmed leader, has a group of senior leaders – the Anglicans call them Canons, the Charismatics, Elders. I will refrain from all word-plays and anecdotal comment, which I have heard mostly from the lips of senior Anglicans! This group needs to be a team, with different levels of seniority providing a discipling framework into which younger people with different gifts may be brought, providing a balanced support to the leaders' work.

In God's grace, He has spoken to me many times, both with encouragement and warning, from the history of king David. Many years ago, when I was beginning to understand that Church was more than meetings, more than I had previously seen or been involved in, I realised that I must make disciples, prepare people and build a house with God's supernatural help to bring glory to His name.

The Lord had already promised our church that it would be a light on a hill and that many people would stream to it. He had said that, "Our branches would go over the wall" (*cf.* Genesis 49:22). We were further thrilled to know that Charles Wesley had confessed the same promise we were believing for our city in 1743, saying, "Surely the Lord hath much people in this place."[1]

To what sort of people was this scripture referring? God gave me a clue in 1976: "*I will increase you with many experienced soldiers*" (1 Chronicles 11 GNB). As I sought to disciple the people God had entrusted into my care, He said He would bring me men and women with experience and ability, and join them to the body, bone to bone, vision to vision. How exciting! How challenging! And more than thirty years later, I can add, "How painful! How delightful! How rewarding!" In fact, all these feelings and more, sometimes all at the same time.

There are many crowds recorded in the Bible, but a crowd is not Church. A valley of dry bones becoming a standing army: maybe that's a better picture of Church (Ezekiel 37). The rabble that came out of Egypt in the great exodus was soon an organised, disciplined community of identified tribes, each with its own position and responsibility: maybe that's Church. The fiery, newly Spirit-filled disciples of the first church in Acts 2 developed a proper structure and leadership roles, appointing "*Men full of faith and of the Holy Spirit*" (Acts 6:5) to "*wait on tables*" (Acts 6:2): *that's* Church. History records that the early churches were dynamic operations, displaying the power of God, reaching out across frontiers, and then challenging and changing the structure of society. "Moreover, the church at the time of writing of this masterful epistle [Romans] must have been a very large and impressive one, because when the frightful persecution under Nero broke loose [AD 63] the Christians were, 'An immense multitude.'"² *That's* Church.

Let us return to the experienced leaders God had promised me. What must I do with them? How do I make them into a team? I somehow knew that the right leadership would build Church. The prophet was the key in Ezekiel; Moses was the leader in the exodus; the Ephesians 4 ministries – apostles, prophets, evangelists, pastors and teachers – were the leaders of the developing first century churches. I had seen few good examples of *team* and had heard many bad accounts of trusted leaders splitting churches, but God had promised me many experienced soldiers and I was already making disciples.

One Monday afternoon, reading a different version of the Bible for a change of emphasis, I read that it was in the power of the King to bring back exiles (2 Samuel 14:14 GNB). The NIV says,

> "But God does not take away life; instead He devises ways so that a banished person may not remain estranged from Him."

The Holy Spirit made it clear to me that it was my responsibility to welcome back a brother who for five years had worked with my father and me until a breakdown in our relationship resulted in his leaving the Nottingham church. A further five years had passed, during which time we had very little contact, but the Spirit of God had already alerted some other leaders that something needed to happen. I argued with God about the matter (I always lose, but still argue, although now only very occasionally). "I don't like the illustration. This 2 Samuel 14 scripture is about Absalom, and the reconciliation did not work out successfully," I protested. I was conscious of the voice of the Spirit saying, "Read on, and I will show you how the reconciliation could have worked out."

1. David did not bring Absalom back with dignity.

> "He must go to his own house; he must not see my face."
> (2 Samuel 14:24)

2. David did not give him a clearly defined role with responsibility, so Absalom made his own role.

> "He would get up early and stand by the side of road leading to the city gate." (2 Samuel 15:1–6)

3. David did not have fellowship with Absalom.

> "Absalom lived for two years in Jerusalem without seeing the King's face." (2 Samuel 14:28)

I obeyed the Lord and brought my friend back with dignity, gave him a proper role with responsibility and maintained regular fellowship with him. Our relationship has since continued for many years to our mutual benefit, only faltering once for a short period when we neglected the third principle and paid the price for our lack of fellowship. This man is an experienced leader, twenty years older than myself. He is a bachelor, he was a salesman and is altogether different in gift and temperament. The Lord knew what He was doing! How enriched my life and ministry have been with this man as part of our leadership team.

It would be easy to fill pages with the joys and sorrows of team construction. Some team members excel beyond expectation while others don't reach their maximum potential. Allowing gifted people to move on to new ministries can be a painful wrench, even when one knows it is God's will. Later on, however, you see in them the fruit of a developed ministry and rejoice. Allow me a side comment about dreams before we continue. Many people have day-dreams, fancy ideas not inspired by a God-given revelation. We must *break the dread* of all such ideas and leave them behind. Some people have dreams which they are confident were sent from God. Sometimes these don't come to fulfilment. The boy marries someone else, the building is sold to a pagan, the gifted friend goes to work with another ministry. In modern language, the dream has passed its "sell-by date". The dream is dead and dead things begin to smell. What must you do? *Bury the dead.* The Christian God is the only One who knows His way out of the grave. If the dream is to live again, God alone must provide it with resurrection life and energy. Others know that what God has promised is still theirs. *"Though it linger, wait for it; it will certainly come and will not delay"* (Habakkuk 2:3) is their confession. *Believe the dream.*

> *"Do not throw away your confidence; it will be richly rewarded. You need to persevere so that when you have done the will of God, you will receive what He has promised."* (Hebrews 10:34–36)

I am still believing, but I have also buried the dead and broken the dread of fanciful ideas.

Notes

1. Wesley, C., quoted in Wylie's *Old and New Nottingham*, p. 130, *cf.* Acts 18:10.
2. Bartlett, C.N., *Romans*, Moody Press, 1953.

Destined to Win

We return to our theme of constructing a team. Different gifts, personalities with varying levels of maturity, direction from God, and a willingness to change are all basic ingredients in team building. Combine these in an atmosphere of love, trust and affirmation, and we have made a start in providing a foundation at leadership level that bodes well for the building of something substantial. But what are the characteristics required for good leadership? How do you know who to choose? And how do we continue developing new talent? Let us examine each of these important questions separately.

In answer to the first question, "What characteristics are required for good leadership?" we must state some of the basic qualities highlighted in Scripture. In a world high on the X-Factor and low on moral qualities it is important to remind ourselves that for Bishops, otherwise called overseers (1 Timothy 3:2–7), the requirements are much more to do with integrity than ability, presence or charisma. Firstly then, we are looking for good people whom God has chosen.

If Christianity is "being like Jesus", then leaders should follow His example most closely. Jesus said that He *did not come to be served, but to serve* (Matthew 20:28). To the amazement of the disciples, after washing their feet He told them,

> *"Now that I, your Lord and Teacher, have washed your feet, you also should wash one another's feet. I have set you an example that you should do as I have done for you."*   (John 13:14–15)

A servant attitude is therefore a fundamental requirement in all those who aspire to be a part of a leadership team. This attitude is not first an activity, but a condition of the heart which affects thinking, planning and action.

> *"Each of you should look not only to your own interests, but also to the interests of others."*   (Philippians 2:4)

A tough scripture indeed. "God will never give you a vision of your own until you have served someone else's vision", was a bold statement I once heard. Loyalty and commitment to a leader's vision, reflected in hard work and enthusiasm, is another basic prerequisite.

In choosing new leaders, always listen to the witness of the Holy Spirit. You may be confident about the person's gift and ability, but lack the overall peace of God regarding the matter. I have found this warning, this check, this unsettling of what I know in my spiritual "knower", to be untiringly correct. To choose leaders contrary to the wisdom of the Spirit is to court disaster. A little more time taken in preparation and in choosing can save a lot of pain and damage later on.

"How do you know who to choose?" you may ask. If you are satisfied with their character, ask yourself, "Who is already using initiative and showing aptitude?" Train and develop those people.

"How do we develop new talent?" was the third question. It is always wise to look at Jesus. What did He do? He obviously prayed because He only ever did what His father told Him to do (John 5:19; 5:30). This is a good place to start. Mark 3:13–15 says that Jesus,

"Called to Him those He wanted, and they came to Him. He appointed twelve – designating them apostles – that they might be with Him and that He might send them out to preach and to have authority to drive out demons."

There are several clear steps here from which we may learn.

1. He called those He wanted
It is important that leaders affirm the people they call to work with them. They should want to be together. I have seen so many groups and teams who obviously don't even like each other, let alone want to be together!

2. They came to Him
A decision to stand alongside the one who calls is important.

3. He appointed twelve – designating them apostles
A clear role is important: it may develop and change, but be as specific as possible in identifying gift and function.

4. . . . That they might be with Him
So many senior leaders fail here. A great deal of good discipling organically happens when "the called" are with their leader. In this process Jesus took, taught, trained and trusted His disciples. I am often saddened when I hear younger leaders lamenting that the relationship with their seniors is purely professional. No time is spent in helping them to be better people, more able leaders, stronger communicators and preachers. They should be built up, helped to do better, and encouraged to achieve excellence – just call it "making disciples".

5. . . . That He might send them out to preach
A missionary once said, "The power is in the going." We must prepare people to go and preach.

6. . . . *And to have authority to drive out demons*

Many leaders have no experience of the authority of Jesus in the supernatural realm – some because of an inadequate theology, others because no one has trained them. Jesus had obviously prepared His disciples. Speaking to the group of seventy-two, He instructed them to preach, *"The kingdom of God is near you"* (Luke 10:9), and to expect the miraculous. They returned to Him with joy: *"Lord, even the demons submit to us in your name,"* they said (Luke 10:17). He told them to rejoice instead that their names were written in heaven (Luke 10:20). He had prepared and trained them very well.

A further look at the twelve reveals that Jesus had used different methods in calling them to Himself. How gratifying that the Saviour treated them as individuals, valued them and called each in an appropriate way. I am so pleased that the gospel of God's love and grace does not endeavour to make uniformed clones and faceless robots of us, but rather releases the full potential of every unique individual. What Good News! The call to *"Follow me"* was issued to Simon in a wonderfully sensitive but demanding way (Luke 5:1–11). I am quite sure that Jesus knew exactly how He intended the encounter to end, but He began so gently.

> *"He got into one of the boats, the one belonging to Simon, and asked him to put out a little from the shore."*   (Luke 5:3)

It was so easy for Simon to cooperate; he was delighted to be identified with this crowd-puller. Jesus was the focus of all gathered at the lake and Simon was in the boat with him! Maybe the first step in being a disciple is to let Jesus into your boat, be it your business or your livelihood. He wants to sit in your everyday circumstances, where you make a living. Then come some more challenging instructions: *"Put out into deep water and let down the net for a catch"* (verse 4). This was more difficult for Simon, since it focused on last night's failure and demanded honesty and a new level of faith. *" . . . but because you say so I will let down the nets"* (verse 5), he replies nonetheless. Does following Jesus make you focus on past failure in spite of hard work? You could ignore His challenge, but somehow His words inspire faith in you and forward you go.

Simon then experienced a miracle of provision – so many fish that the boat was sinking! With his partners they landed the catch and Simon fell to his knees repenting and confessing his wretched state: *"Go away from me, Lord; I am a sinful man!"* (verse 8). The drama ends with Jesus calling him to his life's work: *"Don't be afraid; from now on you will catch men"* (verse 10). And so, pulling the boats on shore, Simon and his friends *"left everything and followed him"* (verse 11).

I've briefly described Simon Peter's journey through identification, obedience and repentance to following the Galilean peasant who was the Son of God. He subsequently had many hard experiences, but I am confident he never regretted the decision which he had made to follow Jesus. All the other disciples had their own special story to tell. I have my own. I trust and pray that you too have met and are following Jesus. The call to follow Him is the greatest call of all. In its message are many secrets. We would do well to learn them, for they will help us to treat people as individuals and to make good disciples.

When you read the gospels it is soon apparent that the individuality of the disciples expressed itself through their personalities, temperaments and abilities. One is looking after the money, another asking questions, yet another is a spokesman; they are all so different. What gifts should we be looking for when building a team of leaders? It makes sense to have variety: not everyone is gifted at looking after the money! (Incidentally, do make sure that your finance people have *faith*. This is more important than their ability to count!) We can't have everyone asking questions, since we also need some answers. We do need, however, some who ask the hard questions: Why? When?

Where? What? and How Much? Not everyone can be a spokes-man; we get confused enough without a multi-mouthed monster speaking a variety of messages to the people.

Once in an overseas situation, I spent some time with a team of three experienced and godly men who have been super-naturally drawn together for a national work. The momentum of their coming together has sustained a successful ministry, but the success is demanding changes. One man is a committed, out-and-out hard-driving adventurer. He is only interested in answers, in advancing. He would say, in David Livingstone's words, "Onwards, anywhere, provided it be forward." The oldest of the three of them is a spiritual man who thinks deeply and is always full of questions, many of them being the right and necessary "next questions". Thankfully, number three stands between Mr Answers and Mr Questions, and it is just as well that he does, because without help these two won't have a strong relationship. Our man-in-the-middle by temperament, training and gift is a wise, even-tempered man who has understanding for, and enjoys a good relationship with, both of the others. If they can learn to draw on each others' strengths and compensate for each others' weaknesses, they will form a powerful team. This is the ideal situation for a successful leadership group. Any alternative is a cocktail of explosives.

Who's on the Team Sheet?

In a study on management, R. Meredith Belbin suggests that an effective team might consist of eight people with different giftings working on four axes (see diagram on the next page). Each person within the team is designated a different title expressing their function. The "plant" and "monitor" evaluators provide the thinking axis, while control is furnished by the "chairman" and "shaper". Information handling and communication are supplied by the "completer-finisher" and a "resource investigator", and the final axis of action is generated by the "company worker" and "team worker".[1]

As I look around the table at my senior leadership meetings, names can so easily be attributed to many of Belbin's team roles. It is only one man's model, but is worthy of some thought and exploration. Tom Marshall, looking specifically at the evaluation of goals, says,

> "One of the strengths of team leadership, an eldership for example, is that members of the team will probably tackle the process of evaluation from several different perspectives, so that a proposal has to pass a fairly searching scrutiny to gain approval. Here are some of the likely perspectives:
>
> *1. The Analyst*
> This is the person who always breaks a thing down into its constituent parts, considers the characteristics of each and finds

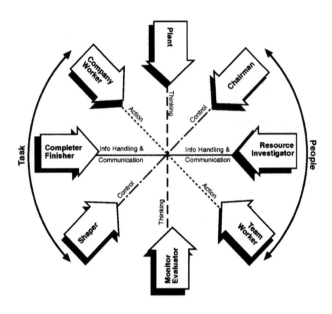

out how the parts relate to the whole. He takes complex
ideas apart as precisely as he takes an intricate mechanism to
pieces.

2. The Assessor

Value, merit, worth, importance and significance are the categories in which this person customarily thinks. Sometimes the
conclusions are arrived at as the result of a quick once-over; at
other times they are reached after the methodical application
of specific criteria. Practicality, quality, authenticity and cost
effectiveness are the assessor's main interests.

3. The Calculator

This is the person who likes to work toward exact quantitative
or predictive determinations; therefore he thinks in terms of
budget projections, cost estimates or quantifiable results. He
wants to see figures, not just vague ideas.

4. The Monitor
The monitor usually focuses on how things measure up to recognised standards or established criteria. A proposal will therefore be evaluated in relation to previous decisions or precedents or the way in which it harmonises with, or deviates from, the policies that have already been set, or those set by other relevant authorities.

5. The Intuitive
This person's evaluative capacity is characterised by intuitive insight and shrewd discernment. He or she has the ability to see through appearances, to stand in the other person's shoes, to discern their needs, problems and expectations and to anticipate what they are likely to do. In situations where people's interests predominate, or where there is the need for the kind of discernment that leads to effective strategising in dealing with others, the intuitive person shines.

6. The Judge
This person is motivated to make decisions or choices based on an even handed weighing up of the pros and cons of a course of action or a rational examination of the relative merits of alternative policies. Once all the pertinent information or views have been laid out, he or she reviews them and sorts them out in accordance with their strong and weak points. In other words, the judge is the person who generally brings the discussion to a head and insists that some decision be made."[2]

If we believe that Jesus is building His Church (and we do) then we must also believe that He sends His Spirit to lead us into all truth. The three Messianic anointings that Isaiah declares make plain that the Spirit of the Lord provides an anointing to proclaim the year of the Lord's favour: the Jubilee (Isaiah 61). I have heard Jubilee described in this way: "I get what belongs to me, you get what belongs to you and God gets what belongs to

Him." Sounds good to me! In Isaiah 42:3 the Spirit's anointing is to *"bring forth justice."* Thankfully, the Church is again responding to this anointing. The first of the Messianic anointings recorded in Isaiah 11:2 declares,

> *"The Spirit of the LORD will rest on him –*
>> *the Spirit of wisdom and of understanding,*
>> *the Spirit of counsel and of power,*
>> *the Spirit of knowledge and of the fear of the LORD."*

Therefore, good judgement and wise decisions come from the Spirit of God. I suggest that after our careful planning, evaluation and assessment, our first and final dependency is on the Spirit of God who will guide us, bring the right people to us, and protect us from making mistakes as we stay filled and dependent on Him.

The Proverbs further show that wisdom is the principal thing (Proverbs 4:7 KJV), illustrating this in the statement,

> *"By wisdom a house is built, and through understanding it is established; through knowledge its rooms are filled with rare and beautiful treasures."*   (Proverbs 24:3–4)

To give greater strength to the argument the writer adds,

> *"A wise man has great power,*
>> *and a man of knowledge increases strength;*
> *for waging war you need guidance,*
>> *and for victory many advisers."*   (Proverbs 24:5–6)

The book of Ecclesiastes teaches that in a small city besieged by a powerful king lived,

> *"A man poor but wise, and he saved the city by his wisdom . . . So I said, 'Wisdom is better than strength.'"*   (Ecclesiastes 9:15–16)

Paul instructs us that,

> *"You are in Christ Jesus, who has become for us wisdom from God."*
>
> (1 Corinthians 1:30)

God Himself works as a team, as manifested in the operation of the Trinity. We recognise the need to be in *team*, but are faced with the question, "How is *team* built?" Over the years in which I have been involved in church leadership, four stages in the evolution of *team* have become clear to me. I am very conscious in describing these stages that many other possibilities arise, especially when working with existing teams or long established elderships and groups, but I am confident that the principles are very relevant.

1. Dependence

The leader calls new people. Sometimes they have experience, but frequently will be new leaders with huge potential, energy and – like the rest of us – plenty to learn. These new team members are highly dependent upon their leader. They are new to their role and want the affirmation and direction of the leader as they gain experience and become strong and confident in their anointing and gifts. Time passes and their ministry is successful. I have often thought about the two statements recording the development of Jesus:

> *"The child grew and became strong; He was filled with wisdom, and the grace of God was upon him."* (Luke 2:40)

and,

> *"Jesus grew in wisdom and stature, and in favour with God and men."*
>
> (Luke 2:52)

I am disappointed if this process is not visible in developing leaders. Their success takes us to the next stage.

2. Counter-dependence

Let me use an illustration of the change from dependence to counter-dependence. A young man with a servant heart, boundless energy and an obvious call to ministry was given the opportunity to lead a youth and children's programme. At first he was very nervous about taking the initiative; he was a good decision-maker but needed to develop confidence. He was eager to please and genuinely wanted to be submissive. His energy, attitude, the gift of God in him and much more caused this work to succeed. In the years since those first nervous steps, several people have come to work full-time under his leadership. Currently, 7,000 children are hearing the Gospel in infant and primary schools every term. Hundreds of children gather each week to be taught in homes around the city. Poor children are given special holidays and treats. Many young people are becoming Christians and are being baptised and discipled. Children from church families are taught the Word of God and the love of Christ is making an impact on many university students. This young man now has at least 150 leaders and workers in the many youth and children's departments, all answerable to his leadership, and I am now dependent on him for the efficient running of all these ministries.

As I look more widely at the church, I ask how the many cell group ministries continue to prosper and be blessed. What about our missionary work in the world? I can not run the social action programmes, visit the prisons or carry out the ministry to the senior citizens. Who is pastoring the people under my care? Who is watching over the crisis counselling and hospital visiting? Who is making sure that the many prayer initiatives are successful, and who is involved in teaching our students and arranging relevant Bible teaching programmes for the people of God? We are committed to the education of our children, but who is doing the work? As the leader I am counter-dependant on many others, especially the senior leaders who work with me, to ensure the successful running of these and many other programmes.

3. Independence

Now that this team of leaders is relatively mature and confident with obvious evidence of the blessing of God, many of them do not need the same affirmation and supervision; they are capable of working alone. One challenge which may arise is when successful team members leave to go and run another ministry. If their departure is handled properly then their entry into this new phase of life will be successful, but so many ministries are not mature enough to deal with this level of change which involves giving away experienced soldiers. Another challenge comes in the handling of confrontation without conflict. In these situations, many issues can remain unresolved, either through mutual respect, fear or independence. Often that which at first sight appears to be *team* is revealed, upon closer inspection, to be a group of individuals all doing their own thing with little or no regard for the wellbeing of each other or for the overall success of the team's vision and purpose. Each member is given a fancy title, but the whole work is compartmentalised, and all go insane watching the work destroy itself! Stumbling at these and other challenges, few teams reach and enjoy the fourth and final phase.

4. Interdependence

In this situation, each team member is valued for his or her gift, experience and ability. All are committed to the success of the others. Strengths and weaknesses are recognised and help is given as required. The vision of the whole is kept firmly in view by all the team. Clear recognition and honour are given to the anointed leader whose job it is to maintain equilibrium within the team whilst ensuring momentum. This will bring success. There are not enough of these teams around. An abundance of them would enable stronger foundations to be built and greater work to be accomplished, rendering greater glory to God in the building of His House in any community or nation. The Church of Jesus would have more opportunity to be the fullness of Him who fills everything in every way.

Notes

1. Belbin, R.M., *Management Teams – Why They Succeed or Fail*, Heinemann.
2. Marshall, T., *Understanding Leadership*. Sovereign World, Chichester, 1991, p. 27.

The Game Plan

Let me illustrate the development of *team* in a diagrammatic form, extrapolating the management principles first conceived by John Adair. *Team* comprises the Leader, a clear Purpose, and will only work properly if there is a strong sense of Fellowship and, hopefully, friendship.

It is quite obvious from looking at the general mêlée of society that groups of people gather together around each of these focal points. The local pub, social club and much of church life is built around the friendship/fellowship criterion. Diagrammatically we now show fellowship as a developed focus, while purpose and leadership are weak.

The next possibility is that groups, or even teams, are built round the focus of a purpose. Many environmental lobbies, political groups and highly motivated "evangelistic" groups begin with a purpose. In our diagram the purpose is dominant and leadership and fellowship are weak.

The third option is a leadership-driven team or group, built around a gifted leader. The diagram shows leadership as strong, but purpose and fellowship are weak.

If we understand that successful team is three equally emphasised interrelating areas . . .

. . . which of the above options have the most possibility of achieving success? If we take the Church as an example, we see that there are many fellowship-driven groups. This includes many small local churches, fraternals and committees which are content to have only fellowship. Fellowship is perfectly right and proper in its place, but it has the power to suffocate progress if it is too dominant. Groups based on fellowship therefore rarely develop good leadership and have only a limited understanding of purpose.

Here is an example. XYZ is a town of 20,000 people. An elder at one of the few "live" churches, when challenged about the state of the fifty-member-strong congregation, expressed his pleasure at the condition of his happy community. At worst this could be interpreted to mean, "Let the majority go to hell, who cares anyway!" Weak leadership with no real purpose yields only a "happy little church".

The Pharisees were a purpose-driven group. A strong doctrinal belief was their point of common interest. Purpose-based groups, gathered for whatever reason, seldom develop strong leadership and can only offer limited fellowship. Crusaders, whether impaled by a doctrinal interest, or an environmental or governmental belief, don't usually build strong *team*.

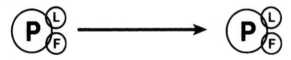

For the sake of balance, it is important that I make two observations immediately. Firstly, that our doctrine is of great importance: that which you believe dictates the way in which you live. The Bible instructs us to *"watch your life and doctrine closely"* (1 Timothy 4:16), and as a leader I am required to impart a proper belief system and lifestyle to those whom I am discipling. Secondly, the world is filled with two kinds of people: reasonable people and unreasonable people. Only the "unreasonable" people have the will to change things. This must mean that there is a place for some crusaders, people of unique intent and individuality of thought. Would we enjoy the blessings of the Reformation without such crusaders? However, in terms of team building it is still the case that purpose-based groups don't usually develop to their full potential.

Jesus Christ was the greatest man who ever lived. His team developed from His leadership. We have already observed that He called and chose His disciples and then proceeded to mould them to His purpose. When each of the twelve were called they had little or no understanding of the enormity of the task set before them. Within the group some were relatives or friends, but fellowship was still an unresearched concept. They had many failures – let us call them learning experiences – during their years with Jesus, and they all greatly disappointed Him around the time of His death. Despite this, once empowered by the Holy Spirit at Pentecost, the years of development and input from Jesus revealed a new maturity in them. They went and turned the world upside down, and many of them are thought to have been martyred for their faith and commitment to Jesus Christ. The leadership-driven team, in my estimation, offers the greatest possibility of developing to its highest potential.

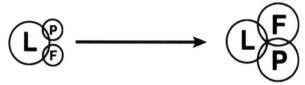

In the days of the judges and kings of Israel, the leaders were a key factor in determining the moral direction of the people of God and in the life of the nation. It has always been so and is still true today. The leader's anointing from and appointment by God (Ephesians 4:11) is recognised in its proper place; in a cathedral this is represented by the *cathedra*, the bishop's chair. The team of leaders is gathered around it; in the cathedral these people are the Canons, each with their unique contribution to make. How can this team achieve its goals? How do we motivate the different personalities? How do we make sure that we all pull together?

What's the Result?

A friend of mine ran a business with a turnover of millions of pounds each year. Sometimes there were cash-flow problems and his bank manager would become edgy. His nervousness occasionally found very specific expression, being vocalised in terms such as, "You must deposit £40,000 by 4:30 pm!" On several occasions a customer with a physical or spiritual need came onto the business premises. My friend, Terry, would think nothing of spending an hour or more to help them. Why? Partly because he believed that in honouring God by sharing his faith, the Lord would help him in the needs of the business (and countless times God indeed proved faithful), but also because Terry is a people person, whom some psychologists would describe as an "affiliator". Other people I know are motivated in different ways. They may be list-writers, staying focused all the time; there are outstanding items on their list and achievement is their motivation. "Let me get my job done," they say. A further group is excited by making decisions. These people are inspired and motivated by seeing projects set in motion. "Let's get the job started," is their cry.

Human beings are not simply machines programmed for action; nevertheless it is wise to develop an understanding of different people's motivation. Few people have only one focus; most are stronger in two of the above three categories. One of the key leaders who works with me scores high on all three counts. Helping the affiliators to work with people, the achievers to work on tasks and the power people to make decisions will provide drive, motivation and enthusiasm, as well as creating a naturally and spiritually comfortable place to work in.

Generating an atmosphere where teamwork is demonstrably productive is important. Being a team player yourself and leading by example is also important. When people realise the truth of the Bible statement . . .

> *"Two are better than one,*
> *because they have a good return for their work."*
>
> (Ecclesiastes 4:9)

. . . they will be more enthusiastic to work together, even though it is a costly business. The picture of two great shire horses harnessed together, straining every sinew, has a strange beauty. It is a fact that a harnessed pair can pull more than the sum of two shire horses pulling individually.

From Trent Bridge in Nottingham you can often see oarsmen training, developing strength, understanding and rhythm. The "togetherness" and fluid movement of a full boat as it glides through the water is a picture worth remembering when you are tempted to forget the other people you work with and strike out on your own. Paul wrote, *"We are God's fellow workers"* (1 Corinthians 3:9), expressing the idea that we work together with Him. The Greek word used for "working together" is *synergos* from which we derive the word "synergy". It's true that two are better than one. Cooperating with God is the greatest team setting for anyone, and working with each other and with God is a three-fold cord that cannot easily be broken (Ecclesiastes 4:12).

Remember what my friend John Shelbourne said about "seeing together and flowing together"? This term implies more than a pragmatic knowledge that *team* is efficient; it is more than the truth of synergy; it is more than the encouragement of the Bible stories of *team*. Each of us needs a revelation in order to see the corporate vision. We need to see that God has anointed leaders in every generation for every level of his work:

"Officials over thousands, hundreds, fifties and tens."

(Exodus 18:21)

We need to see that all these leaders should make disciples, develop teams around them, bring to maturity and release into service the diverse talents in the great people who make up the Body of Christ. With this leadership foundation laid, significant progress can be made in building the house, the habitation of God, the Cathedral. Just as in the natural realm, these huge stone edifices that stand in the heart of many of our older cities remind us of their past and present influence in most areas of society, so perhaps in the spiritual realm we will begin to see huge buildings of living stones, growing strongly in the heart of urban decay and hopelessness to bring the *"light of the glory of Christ"* (2 Corinthians 4:4) back to the centre of our communities, touching and influencing every sector of modern society in a relevant way which brings hope. If you don't see this vision for yourself, you will not flow together with like-minded people to embrace it and make it a reality.

On many occasions I have travelled to Manaus, Brazil, in the heart of Amazonia. The very first time I visited, in the mid-nineties, it was a joy to observe a great move of God with thousands of people following the Lord Jesus. At the same time I was overcome with gratitude to God. He had promised me as a young man that if I sought first the Kingdom of God and His righteousness then all other things would be given to me (Matthew 6:33). Geography and the natural world have been a fascination since my boyhood days and here, yet again, God was proving faithful to His promise: I was to see another of the places I had read about as a boy, and it happened, as usual, in the process of serving the Lord.

We flew one day, by a single-engined Cessna, to one of the riverside churches in a journey which takes thirty minutes by plane or eighteen hours by boat. Once the morning's work was over we headed back to Manaus through a storm. Before landing we were flown over the confluence of the great Amazon river where the Solimões and Negro rivers meet. The separating bank ends, but the rivers continue as two distinct streams in the same channel for a considerable distance, the dark water of the Negro being easily distinguished from the lighter, muddy-coloured Solimões. I asked the pilot why this phenomenon occurred. "There are three reasons," he answered. "Firstly, the constitutions of the rivers are very different; secondly, the rivers flow at different speeds; and thirdly, the waters are at different temperatures." He turned the plane back to the city, but my mind was now thinking about his interesting remarks. After we as leaders have "seen" a new revelation, grasped a principle, or come to understanding, we must be careful to bring the team members and then our people up to speed. We must take time to bring everyone (or as many as will respond) to the same level of enthusiasm and desire, and give time for the different personalities to mix their ideas and assessments together. Then we will not only see together but also flow together in the same way that the Solimões and Negro rivers do, eventually blending into one after many miles.

One of the obvious signs of togetherness in a successful sports team is noise. Team members shout to, for and at each other, be it information, encouragement or rebuke. They show a strong commitment to each other and to their cause, and we should learn from this. A similar illustration is that of geese flying long distances. When a skein of geese fly south for the winter, the V-formation they adopt serves more purpose than impressive aerobatics. The range of the flock is increased by at least seventy percent since the drag and air resistance to each goose is dramatically reduced due to the aerodynamics involved. All the geese in the skein are continually honking, calling to one another to keep in formation, to keep going, making such a noise that they can be heard long after they have passed from sight. When the lead goose gets tired from flying at the point of the V, he drops back and another goose flies point. Finally, should a goose fall sick or become wounded or exhausted, two other geese leave the formation with it. Only once it has recovered or died will they recommence their journey south.

The challenge comes to us from this analogy: if we have as much sense as a goose, we will work together to achieve more, stay in formation with those who are headed the same way as we are going, take our turn doing the hard work, consider carefully what we call out from behind, and stand by each other.[1]

At regular intervals we gather together all those who function in leadership roles within the life of the church. On one such occasion we decided that we would not hold "another leaders' night", but that this night would be different. Coffee helped the atmosphere, the jazz quintet played their part, and senior leaders welcomed each person as they arrived. It was winter, so overcoats were taken and carefully hung. Everything was designed to say, "You're welcome, we appreciate you, and we're glad you are here and are involved with us in this work." The lighting was different and the platform setting was unusual. A fast-moving presentation followed which was humorous, challenging and inspiring. Then it was my turn to say, "Thank you", expressing my appreciation for all the hard work, and to remind people that we could not carry on this scale of ministry without all of them playing their part. We called it a "Honking Night" – remember the illustration of the geese? – everyone shouting, "Keep in line! Stay in place! If we hold formation we can get there!"

Nehemiah recognised that he was *"carrying on a great project"* (Nehemiah 6:3). Jesus said, *"My Father is always at His work to this very day, and I, too, am working"* (John 5:17). Paul said, *"forgetting what is behind and straining towards what is ahead, I press on towards the goal to win the prize for which God has called me heavenwards in Christ Jesus"* (Philippians 3:13–14).

Come on! Lift up the hands that hang down, strengthen the feeble knees. Together in God's strength we can accomplish God's will and we can see the glory of this present house becoming greater than anything that has gone before (Haggai 2:9). But we need each other, whether inside a local community of Christians, in the wider reaches of the Church, or among all the peoples of planet earth. Let us live for the glory of God and build a house in which God lives by His Spirit.

In the next section of the book we will examine how the anointed leader and his team can effectively disciple the whole body. Before looking at this in detail we will review the building of the Cathedral thus far.

Notes

1. Abridged from F. Damazio, *Effective Keys to Successful Leadership.* Bible Temple Publishing, Portland, OR, 1993, p. 42.

SECTION 3
Discipleship

The Cloisters

You're Mad!

The closing verses of Ephesians 2 dramatically describe the Church as a magnificent, holy temple with *"Christ Jesus Himself as the chief cornerstone"* (Ephesians 2:19–22). Jesus said He would build His Church (Matthew 16:18). The writer to the Hebrews speaks of God as an architect and builder (Hebrews 11:10). The Bible outlines the plan to ensure that thousands of people – living stones – are built together to become a dwelling for God. If these and other similar biblical comments are true, and they undoubtedly are, then why does so much of Western Christianity fall short of God's glorious ideal? There are many visionless congregations barely managing to survive. Some churches are nothing more than a collection of people who have little or no sense of community, and no discipling or development strategy. We can also see the other extreme in physical edifices, both ancient and modern, that are high on style but, sadly, low on content. The only conclusion we can arrive at is that we cannot be following the Master Builder's instructions properly.

Looking particularly at Britain, and even allowing for the disruption of the great wars, much of the Christian Church has fostered a survivalist, insular mentality which has greatly suppressed our potential. Most of our buildings have been small; many of them characterless. A building made to seat 500 people is thought of as large. The whole scenario speaks of limited vision and an acceptance of the fallacy that we are doomed to remain a small minority. Please look again at the Master's plans!

When we make a decision to build something – be it a house, a factory, a church, or whatever we desire to construct – there are certain basic principles that are essential for a successful project. We must first obtain the proper plans and permission; we need to ensure that we are building on the right foundations; and then we may eventually see something satisfactory above ground level. The foundations are so important. Their size and quality will predict the eventual size of the completed building. Of course, we need the agreed permission to allow these foundations to be put in place, and we receive that permission because the plans have been drawn and approved by the Head of the Church. Remember that the building of the people of God is to be the fullness of Him who fills everything in every way. The Church is designed to be a glorious entity. Jesus said,

> *"I will put together my Church, a Church so expansive with energy that not even the gates of hell will be able to keep it out."*
>
> (Matthew 16:18, *The Message*)

The builders of the cathedral in Salisbury, England, decided in 1402 to build something so great that those who followed would think them mad to have even attempted it. That was a literal building, but we must capture the vision and enthusiasm to see the building of living stones rising up: millions of people who were spiritually dead, inwardly longing to be forgiven, becoming an integral part of something significant and fulfilling; something eternal. As we realise this greater vision, our physical buildings will reflect it as thousands more people turn to Christ. An increase of interdenominational and inter-church activities, and a zeal to plant new churches, are all part of a recaptured vision of the Church of Jesus Christ, built as He wants it.

As previously stated, the right plans and permission are essential in order to start building, but let us focus on the foundational aspect in a little more detail as we conclude this section of our journey. The Apostle Paul insists that Jesus Christ is the chief cornerstone of the building (Ephesians 2:20; cf. 1 Peter 2:4–7). He also maintains that apostles and prophets are part of the Church's foundations. Without these "sent" builders and seers the foundations will not be as strong or expansive as the Master Builder requires and the potential to build will be limited immediately.

Strengthening and enlarging already existing foundations is an expensive, disruptive and sometimes dangerous business, so it makes sense to build them to the required size and strength in the initial stages. Progress will then be significantly improved.

I do not believe that the apostles and prophets stand alone, but they are catalytic in the gathering, guiding and releasing of the other Ephesians 4:11 gifts (evangelists, pastors and teachers). A modern-day danger seems to be that those who are essentially pastors and teachers are too often attempting to fulfil apostolic and prophetic leadership roles, while the evangelist is often viewed as a maverick-type figure with his own ministry, who belongs everywhere and nowhere at the same time. The true strength of the foundations is only realised when all these gifts and ministries work together in a cohesive group, as previously stated, recognising each other's gift and being able to be guided, inspired and released for the greater benefit of the whole body of believers. Gifted men, working in relationship at this level will provide great strength for the body, a sense of direction and proper fathering which always wants the best for those under their care. What good natural father does not want his offspring to succeed more and do better than himself? Likewise, godly fathering should not be an attempt to build our own kingdoms or ministries. It should be the release of God's Father heart through us, so that every child reaches his or her highest potential and is able to function to the greatest benefit of Christ's Church and the greater glory of God's name.

Most churches in the world are small. This in itself is not a problem; if a church is healthy, it will be growing, reproducing and multiplying – all healthy things grow! Wonderful, but a significant minority of the Western world's small churches are not healthy and are not growing. Why not? At least one reason is that the foundations are incomplete. Many churches have an unbiblical view of leadership. Some are trapped in a one-man-ministry model. What a monstrosity and how peculiar it is to see one person trying to do everything in any sphere of life. Still others are too narrow in their understanding of local church autonomy, not allowing other God-appointed and God-anointed leaders access to speak from a position of relationship and recognition into areas of often obvious need. All these symptoms point to a diagnosis of limited vision, trapped in a certain mindset and way of thinking.

Should every church then, be a huge cathedral with thousands of people? Of course not. Many churches in rural and urban settings need to be family churches, very local and touching their immediate community. But they should all have the Ephesians 4 gifts working in them and make use of those available to them through relationship with other churches. They should all be growing and be a part of the wider gatherings of the Body of Christ. I do believe that there should and will be, speaking of Britain (I believe it to be true of most other places), large cathedral churches, with thousands of people and significant visibility, working with and relating to the many smaller but equally valid expressions of Christ's Body in their region.

Without doubt, in order to grow upwards from strong foundations, we must pull together as a team. The mindset that people hold of "our pastor" or "our minister" leads to false expectations of what this "guru" type figure can and is expected to do. This, together with a limited understanding of *team*, has restricted the spiritual and numerical growth of thousands of churches. As we grow bigger we need to renew our minds and restructure as required – here comes change again. "Constant change is here to stay," was a favourite saying of a dear friend of mine, Alfred Missen. "God never changes, but He is always on the move," says my father, E.J. Shearman. The management of change is one of the greatest challenges to successful living in any and every sphere of life.

My own experience and that of some of my friends reveals a greater understanding of the foundations. Yes, Jesus Christ ever and always. Yes, apostles and prophets working with and releasing the other Ephesians 4 gifts. But we must also add the gifts of administration and helps (1 Corinthians 12:28). The runaway success of the Church after Pentecost meant that it soon needed re-structuring. In Acts 6 the main leaders found themselves increasingly preoccupied with the care and administration of the Church. This is often what happens when a growing church reaches the apparent barrier of around 500 people. The people with leadership, vision and strength of ministry in prayer and the Scriptures find themselves bogged down with administration, however necessary, and become the victims of crisis management with a "fire-fighting" approach to decision making because forward planning has suffered.

Some may say, "But when the Holy Spirit comes, all this organisational approach is washed away." I beg to differ. The pragmatic approach of the New Testament Church of Acts 6 is an example. Within a biblical framework they changed structure and involved people in order to meet their needs. We should do the same.

An "under-strength" foundation will produce a small, weaker building than could be built (1). A New Testament gift-mix team will develop something bigger and stronger (2). Add serving, support, administrative and steering gifts, and together we can be part of a building "not made with hands", bringing glory to God and doing His work on every front (3): the Church of Jesus, doing what it was designed to do and being what it was designed to be. When all this is in place we can move on to the next phase

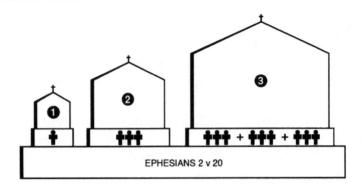

EPHESIANS 2 v 20

of our journey, into the cloisters. The right leadership, working under authority with the right team of gifted leaders and support people, can see the body brought to maturity, ready for the works of service which will be the hands and feet of Jesus to our world. Let's go and make disciples.

I Was Happy Ploughing

A cry from many churches is, "We do not have enough leaders; there are not enough people to do the work." Similarly, Elijah thought that he was *"the only one left"*, but God assured him He had 7,000 others in reserve (1 Kings 19:10). Jethro's advice to Moses that he should select capable men, presupposes, reasonably I think, that a number of people of such a calibre were available (Exodus 18:21). The twelve close confederates, Jesus' apostles, were certainly not all of those being trained; Luke 10 speaks of seventy-two disciples, and in Acts 1 the defined number of followers is 120. When Paul and Barnabas had their disagreement, both easily found other capable people to help them continue their work.

Walking around the historical cloisters of a cathedral, one can imagine a living environment, a working church where the bishop and his key leaders were training and discipling the next generation in an operational environment. There is little room for cold, monastic theory. There is work to be done and experience to be gained.

To my observation, three factors directly influence the effective selection and training of leaders: firstly, the quality and gifts of those involved in the selection of candidates; secondly, the philosophy and programme which is applied to those who are being trained; and thirdly, the quality of general discipleship in the body of believers, which is the limiting factor on the size of the pool of possible candidates.

The Bible records a number of incidents where God retains the initiative in His calling of key leaders, choosing not to involve a human agency. Moses heard the voice of God speaking out of the burning bush. During a startling conversation, God directly commissioned him:

> *"So now, go. I am sending you to Pharaoh to bring my people the Israelites out of Egypt."*   (Exodus 3:10)

Moses was honest, obedient and exercised faith as God provided him with a unique calling card for Pharaoh and the Israelite elders. The New Testament contains an equally remarkable incident. Saul was riding into Damascus only to be confronted by a blinding light. From the ground he answered the voice he heard. *"Who are you, Lord?"* he asked. I am sure he never forgot what he heard next. *"I am Jesus, whom you are persecuting"* (Acts 9:5). Later, a human agent, Ananias, declared prophetically that Saul was God's chosen instrument to carry His name before the Gentiles (Acts 9:15).

These are some of the exceptions to the rule. Many times God uses a human agency as a messenger of His call and purpose. If Elisha was to share his life story, perhaps he would say, "I was happy ploughing, working on the family farm, until that man Elijah threw his cloak over my shoulders." Singing his songs, shepherding his sheep, slinging his stones, would David have recorded in his biography how radically his life changed after he was rushed in from the field to be anointed with oil by Samuel? The Bible says,

> *"From that day on the Spirit of the LORD came upon David in power."*
> (1 Samuel 16:13)

We don't know how the Lord called Amos but we have his confession:

"I was neither a prophet nor a prophet's son, but I was a shepherd, and I also took care of sycamore fig trees. But the LORD took me from tending the flock and said to me, 'Go, prophesy to my people Israel.'"

(Amos 7:14–15)

We have already seen the enormous impact that the words *"Follow me"* made on the disciples of Jesus; in the same vein Paul reminds Timothy,

"Do not neglect your gift which was given you through a prophetic message when the body of elders laid their hands on you."

(1 Timothy 4:14)

History suggests that the likes of the Wesleys, Zinzendorf, Calvin and others were men of gift and destiny who were a magnet to other leaders and trained significant numbers of followers. David Allen tells us how,

Willie Burton and James Salter, defying daunting dangers and privations, pioneered in the Belgian Congo and co-founded the Congo Evangelistic Mission. Zaire now boasts thousands of thriving Pentecostal assemblies built largely upon the foundation of their apostolic labours.[1]

Burton himself (who was, according to my understanding, an apostle) and other senior personnel from his African mission were constantly looking for potential missionary candidates. On their visits to churches they would inspire young men and women with the thrill of serving Jesus. They would speak words of encouragement, and sometimes prophecy would be a factor in the call of God to potential leaders.

I am confident that many more leaders are available in local churches than are ever released. Not enough apostolic and prophetic ministry is being exercised to inspire, excite and challenge the many quality people who have the potential to be

great leaders. They are left using their gift in industry, the pro-
fessions and business. Others remain underdeveloped because
no one saw or spoke to them, and latent talent waiting to be
released was therefore wasted.

I am not for a moment suggesting that every talented person
should be drafted into full-time ministry; many should be encouraged to remain salt and light in the various sectors of society.
Those with a natural ability for making money should be
carefully discipled to release wealth for the work of the Kingdom
of God (cf. 1 Timothy 6:17–19). However, I am suggesting that
many more need to hear the confirming call towards the work
of full-time ministry. Existing leaders are obviously a key to the
success of the next generation coming into ministry.

Many Pentecostal leaders are striking the warning, heard
historically in most of the great revival movements, of the
dangers professionalism, institutionalism and intellectualism
pose to Spirit-filled people. This warning is nowhere more needed
than in every ministry training programme around the world.
No sensible person will argue for ignorance or lack of training,
but is the work of God best served by more and more students
attending longer and longer academically-based programmes?
Of course we need theologians and highly qualified people, but
I am sure that many who take such courses would be better
prepared in shorter, "hands-on" programmes where the training
and discipling are conducted in a working church environment.
If we are to learn from history (and mankind does not have a
good track record in this respect) we will guard with great
diligence against the encroaching tide of professionalism and
intellectualism. Who would have thought that, within twenty
years of Wesley's death, street preachers would be banned by
the Methodists? Or who would believe that only twenty years
after the great revival meetings conducted by Jonathan Edwards,
he would be invited to resign from his church? When in my
youth some of the non-conformist denominations began to
require degree qualification as necessary for ministry, many

Pentecostals declared that they would not make such a decision. Today I would not be so confident. We may acquire knowledge and study to a high level, but it is far more important that we should know an irresistible call from God, be daily filled with the Spirit and live with an experiential understanding of the signs and wonders of the Kingdom of God among us. Jesus illustrated the necessity of this lifestyle when He said,

> *"If I drive out demons by the Spirit of God, then the Kingdom of God has come upon you."*   (Matthew 12:28)

The latent gifts and abilities possessed by so many people remain latent partly because we offer inadequate discipling and training programmes in the life of the local church. Many churches are like an undug mine, with much treasure waiting to be discovered. Other churches still lack a planned beginners' course, in which new Christians are taught, in an unhurried and unthreatening atmosphere, the basics of the Christian life. The third of five warnings in the book of Hebrews identifies "falling away" with an inadequate grasp of elementary truths (Hebrews 5:11–6:12). It is a surprise to me that many churches do not prepare people for marriage and fail to provide teaching about family life. Similarly, problems with sexuality and finance are not confronted with appropriate biblical teaching. Where do people learn about developing Christian character and using the gifts of the Spirit; or where can they gain understanding about prayer and worship? I will address some of these discipleship issues later, but for now I conclude by restating that a better general programme of making disciples would release a larger pool of potential leaders. For instance, more short-term, locally-based ministry training programmes, in addition to, and as an alternative to, existing full-time institutional preparation, and a greater use of Apostolic and Prophetic anointings to inspire and provoke congregations and individuals, would begin to address the problem of our lack of leaders.

After a lifetime of Christian service and almost forty years in full-time ministry, I find it the most rewarding and challenging way of life. After the mantle of Elijah finally came to Elisha (2 Kings 2:13), the river parted and his own miraculous ministry unfolded. Do you think that Elisha sometimes thought back to his days on the farm and thanked God for the opportunity of serving Jehovah, the great covenant God? Let us, the leaders, begin to pass the mantle to the next generation. On, then, with the work of the cloisters where leaders are being groomed and prepared. The ongoing and demanding work of character development must be explained and demonstrated in any "cloisters" programme.

Notes

1. Allen, D., *The Unfailing Stream*. Sovereign World Ltd, Tonbridge, 1994, p. 123. The nation formerly known as Zaire is now the Democratic Republic of Congo.

CHAPTER 1

The Three M's

We have established that one of leadership's functions is communication and development. In the words of Paul to Timothy,

> *"The things you have heard me say in the presence of many witnesses entrust to reliable men who will also be qualified to teach others."*
> (2 Timothy 2:2)

We observe here four linked ministries: Paul, to Timothy, to reliable men, to others.

It is foundational that any leadership sees the discipling, developing and raising up of the next generation of leaders as a priority, but of equal importance is the discipling and developing of the whole body, with each individual realising his or her maximum potential to the glory of God. From this wider mandate will be drawn the people with ministry gifts who will leave . . .

> *" . . . houses or brothers or sisters or father or mother or children or fields for my sake."* (Matthew 19:29)

The whole body, prepared for works of service (Ephesians 4:12) and becoming mature (Ephesians 4:13), must be a clear goal.

This means that leaders should spend most of their time with the best of their people. It also means that each church should re-examine its diary of events. This requires continual reassessment. Rather than meeting for meeting's sake, doing it because we have always done it out of tradition, we must develop a meaningful programme appropriate to the discipling needs of the body.

I will give one simple illustration. Some years ago the pastor of a family church, who had maybe 100 people under his care, asked my advice. He complained that he was being overstretched by a serious outbreak of marital problems in solid families in the church and was rushing from house to house, desperately trying to maintain the people and the church life. What should he do? As I remember, I gave him two pieces of advice.

The first was to recognise the serious possibility of a demonic attack. The Bible says, *"For our struggle is not against flesh and blood"* (Ephesians 6:12), but my observation is that in quite a few churches *it is!* Why? Because we are blind or ignorant of the devil's schemes. Deal with the problem as the Bible prescribes in Ephesians 6:10–18, by putting on the whole armour of God. Some are afraid of the language of spiritual warfare, but handled within biblical guidelines, I personally feel it is part of our duty as Christians.

The second piece of advice I gave to my pastor friend was that he should temporarily stop the church's midweek meetings, gather all the husbands and wives together and give them appropriate teaching: the Bible's view of marriage, the role of the husband, the role of the wife, problem solving, and possibly follow this with some family teaching. Positive faith-filled teaching and an opportunity to ask questions, discuss problems and respond to the Bible's clear teaching will help people to reach maturity. Proactive, planned activity should replace the reactive, unplanned, very tiring, unfulfilling crisis management common to so many churches.

Leadership development can be summarised as the three M's: the Message, the Man and the Ministry. That is concise enough for my purpose. What do I mean by "the Message"? Paul taught us that we must be workmen who correctly handle, or rightly divide, the word of truth (2 Timothy 2:15). The thought behind the original scripture is like the accurate cutting of a cake. "*I am not ashamed of the Gospel of Christ, because it is the power of God for the salvation of everyone who believes*" (Romans 1:16), is another of Paul's ideas. This is the *kerygma*, the message, as proclaimed by a herald.[1]

Romans 12:2 says that we are not to let the world squeeze us into its mould, but the world constantly tries to. Western education for example, has developed with strong roots in Greek culture.

> "*Jews demand miraculous signs and Greeks look for wisdom, but we preach Christ crucified.*"   (1 Corinthians 1:22)

We would call this the "Greek mind", characterised by its continual demand for explanation, the need to understand everything, the desire that all must be reasonable. Add to this the significant gloss given by the age of reason, the so-called period of enlightenment and the outworking of existential philosophies, and one arrives at the shrine of knowledge called "Modern Education". One of my friends has observed, written over the gates of a university, "Knowledge leads to Wisdom". This typifies the Western mind set. Many people are paraded in public life as being "wise" because they have acquired information and knowledge, and possess qualifications to prove it. It is a very dangerous assumption that wisdom should be the product of such a process. The Bible entirely reverses this concept, insisting that wisdom is the *first and principal thing* (Proverbs 4:7 KJV), and that knowledge and understanding flow from wisdom.

This "squeezing" process leaves Western mankind with a numbness, especially in our understanding of the unseen spiritual world. Focusing on gaining information and knowledge can also claim too high a priority in the preparation of future ministry and leadership.

Whether in the local church, or at any level of Bible college training programme, we must understand the *kerygma*. In learning to rightly divide the word of truth, we must not make the modern educationist's mistake of regarding knowledge as the principal thing. Revelation, spiritual insight and the Spirit leading us into all truth are vital balancing features of preparing the message in the man. Perhaps Bible training programmes should be led by prophets supported by teachers?

So we have addressed ourselves to the divine injunction, *"Watch your life and doctrine closely"* (1 Timothy 4:16), but what about the personality, the "man" that is the vessel to carry the truth? The patience of God through the Bible should be a signpost. Watch His painstaking care in the life of Joseph, seventeen years old and very confident; now see him thirty years old, much wiser and very dependent on God. Perhaps consider Moses, forty years old, exceptionally well trained, very secure in his ability. Then, forty years later, he needs miracles and strong encouragement to do what God had prepared him for. Look at David's relentless progress which I have described earlier; or look at Paul, a religious expert with a dramatic testimony. Finally, what about the Christ of God, our Lord Jesus, who spent only one tenth of His life in public ministry – yet what a ministry! These signposts point to character development as one of God's highest priorities in anyone's life, especially those who would be leaders. Here are a few verses relevant to this topic. I wish someone had explained the process behind them to me when I was a young man.

> *"In the course of my life he broke my strength."*   (Psalm 102:23)

> *"For you, O God, tested us;*
> *   you refined us like silver."*   (Psalm 66:10)

"They bruised his feet with shackles,
his neck was put in irons,
till what he foretold came to pass,
till the word of the LORD proved him true." (Psalm 105:18–19)

"He made me into a polished arrow
and concealed me in His quiver." (Isaiah 49:2)

"No discipline seems pleasant at the time, but painful."
(Hebrews 12:11)

I can hear some voices saying, "That's too negative. You must encourage people with the positive aspects of these and other contexts." Yes, I will.

"You brought us to a place of abundance." (Psalm 66:12)

'It [discipline] *produces a harvest of righteousness and peace for those who have been trained by it."* (Hebrews 12:11)

It is a lament that multitudes of present, potential and fallen leaders were not taught or trained by the difficulties of life. They have failed to grasp God's character-building programme. "It's not what is happening to me that matters; it's how I react to what God knows is happening to me that matters," says my wise, long-time friend Phil Hills from Melbourne, Australia.

In a house in Kuala Lumpur I met an anointed servant of God. It was a supernaturally-arranged encounter. We laughed, talked, shared precious things and then prayed for each other. There were words of prophecy spoken. One of the many things said was that God had made my life into a strong javelin, which would reach its target on many occasions to significant effect; some of the implications of this were further described. "Wonderful, thank you for the word of encouragement." Just a minute: stop! Prophecy is one thing, but how does it come to pass? What is the process which makes a life into a javelin?

Of the scriptures quoted above I will dwell briefly on one of them: Isaiah 49:1–2 insists that the call of God is His area of jurisdiction. In other words, He calls, we respond. Then follows a distinct "making".

While making *"my mouth like a sharpened sword"*, the Bible says that *"in the shadow of His hand He hid me"* (Isaiah 49:2). The epistle of James makes clear what problems our mouths and tongues can cause. We must keep a tight rein on the tongue (James 1:26). When I told a congregation they needed to "get the hell out of their mouths" some seemed shocked. But James 3 teaches us that,

> *"The tongue is a fire, a world of evil . . . It corrupts the whole person, sets the whole course of his life on fire, and is itself set on fire by hell."*
>
> (James 3:6)

So yes, let's get that "hell influence" out of our speech. The Bible says that our words are only an overflow from the heart (Matthew 12:34). Our hearts and emotions are affected by our thinking. The Bible instructs us to renew our minds (Romans 12:2) and take captive every thought (2 Corinthians 10:5). Learning to discipline our thoughts, hearts and words, and allowing the transforming power of God to change us, is an ongoing process.

> *"He made my mouth like a sharpened sword."*   (Isaiah 49:2)

Many leaders, because of immaturity in this area, have damaged their ministry, sometimes their people, and for a time God's work.

Secondly, Isaiah uses a different illustration. *"He made me into a polished arrow."* There are three basic parts to an arrow: the flights, which help direction; the shaft, which is the body of the arrow giving it substance; and the head, sharpened for efficient impact. I will use this as a picture to illustrate God's dealings in our lives.

The flights represent our learning sensitivity to the Holy Spirit, giving us direction. The head is the deposit of gift, both natural and spiritual, which gives force and sharpness to ministry. God is exceptionally generous. He is no richer for withholding, no poorer by giving – a statement beyond our understanding. The implication must follow that gifting should never be a problem. The gifts, the *charisma* of God, are available. Our responsibility is to sharpen and become expert in using the gifts God has given us. If the flights are sensitivity to the Spirit and the head is deposited gift, then the shaft must be a developed character. It is with this part that we have all the problems, but God is very patient with us. I am told that in biblical times the method used for making a shaft was to take a relatively straight branch and strip it of twigs, leaves and bark. Then after a prolonged period of saturation it was pegged to the ground and held straight for a long time, exposed to the changing elements. After this straightening work, it was made smooth and polished with oil. Using this illustration in Australia on one occasion, a missionary lady told me that the Aborigines had a very similar method of making spears, preferring to use heat instead of saturation in the straightening process. The analogy is very applicable to character development.

Has God's stripping taken place in your life and ministry? Isaiah said, *"I am ruined."* Moses said, *"Send my brother."* Paul said, *"I no longer live."* Have you ever been trapped, desperate for a change, but unable to move? God is using your circumstances to straighten you out. Warning: if you move too quickly, He will trap you again. Ouch! But after all the straightening comes the smoothing and polishing with the oil of the Spirit. We are ready for action now, only to be restrained by the words of Isaiah again:

"[He] concealed me in His quiver." (Isaiah 49:2)

I remember when Dorothy and I first came to Nottingham. Prior to this I had gained much experience in leading young people and serving in the life of the church, so I could not understand why no opportunities were immediately given to me. Teaching a Sunday School class, being a doorkeeper or a carrier of the offering bag? Nothing. What a frustrating episode! I was hidden in His quiver. I think I understand what it was about now. It would have been better to have understood then. I might have learned much quicker and been more useful much sooner. The Bible offers this advice to all in the arrow factory:

> *"Wait for the LORD;*
> *be strong and take heart*
> *and wait for the LORD."*   (Psalm 27:14)

The moment does come, I can assure you. The nail-damaged hand of our Master reaches for the waiting arrow in the quiver of obscurity, He focuses on the target and sends you on His purpose. What excitement! What a privilege! After a lifetime of Christian service, I still have goose bumps when I remember the call of God coming to me as a sixteen year old boy, and I am still overwhelmed that He is committed to me doing His work, succeeding and hitting the target. My, oh my, it's worth all the preparation.

Now to the final "M": the ministry. I am not referring to some professional priestcraft, an elite group who alone can forgive sins and administer Communion. Do not think that such a mentality only lives in the citadels of conformist Christianity. It is frighteningly alive in Charismatic manifestations of Church in various parts of the world. I have argued strongly for the recognition of anointed leaders in the Body of Christ, but want to express with equal vigour my belief in the priesthood of all believers. The main nouns used in the New Testament to describe "minister" are *diakonos*, servant; *leitourgos*, public servant; and *hyperetes*, "under-rower", meaning any subordinate activity under another's direction. The outstanding example is our Saviour, the Lord Jesus, who said,

> *"Even the Son of Man did not come to be served, but to serve, and give His life as a ransom for many."*   (Mark 10:45)

The King James version gives, *"Not to be ministered unto but to minister,"* as an alternative translation of this verse. Both in person and action all Christians should be servants and ministers. Paul, writing to the Corinthians, says,

> *"He has made us competent as ministers of a new covenant – not of the letter but of the Spirit; for the letter kills, but the Spirit gives life."*
> (2 Corinthians 3:6)

I am sad when I meet capable and gifted people, prepared for ministry in Bible schools, seminaries, para-church training programmes and local churches, who have little or no experience of the life and work of the Spirit, or alternatively, no understanding of God's character development principles – both, in some cases. These people, when released into specific ministry at home or abroad, are sitting targets for the devil. The high fallout rate from ministry, specifically missionary service, reflects the lack of these experiences in people's lives.

There are many people who are trying to minister who have no understanding of, or experience in, casting out demons; no active, visible ability in using the gifts of the Spirit; none of their Goliaths have been dealt with; and they lack knowledge of the Spirit helping them in their weakness (Romans 8:26). We must all have more than a theological understanding of life in the Spirit. We need reality, experience on the ground. The best way is the method used by Jesus while training His disciples, which I spoke of in Chapter 6. The Navigator movement's philosophy, "Tell him why. Show him how. Get him started. Keep him going. Teach him how to pass it on" reflects this excellent model.

The right message, ministered the right way through the right man will put us on track for growing a Cathedral full of big people, who, let loose, will change their world. I have another secret to share with you from creation, which is better than the Big Bang. It develops these big people. Turn the page with care – reading on could affect you!

Notes

1. *Vine's Expository Dictionary of New Testament Words*. Barbour and Co. Inc., Westwood NJ, 1952.

CHAPTER 13

The Secret of Creation

If we were to believe that mankind is some happenstance, some unplanned, irrelevant flotsam, who is here today and gone tomorrow forever, then the concept of humanity's specialness and chosen purpose would, naturally, be impossible to grasp or implement. The need to identify ourselves as part of a planned creation made by a creator God is of fundamental importance. Earlier I spoke of God as a communicator, but He is of course much more. When the Spirit of God moved (the *ruach*, the "breath" of God, as the Hebrew language describes) and God spoke, something was created out of nothing: light (Genesis 1:3).

Whenever the Spirit of God and the Word of God consort, something miraculous happens. Some understanding of this supernatural chemistry, however fragmentary, reveals a view of the greatness of God. His vast omnipotence is manifested by creation. We may marvel at how quickly it all happened; perhaps the angelic kingdom was surprised He was so patient in taking a whole six days! I suppose they had similar feelings watching the events of the resurrection. The disciples were mesmerised with life after death; the angels, content that things were back to normal, were more surprised by the Creator laying down His life in death a few days earlier. So much of our theology and limited understanding belong to human prescription, making God fill the boundaries of our minds and comprehension. We are rarely able to see things from the perspective our Creator sees them. Viewed from one side, a signpost next to the southernmost house on the English mainland may read, "The last house in England". But looking north from the other side, the same house becomes, "The first house in England". Same house, different perspective.

God is God before all things. He is beyond the greatest attempts at definition or inspired literary genius. He is, simply stated, beyond our comprehension. Opening our minds to such concepts of His vastness is part of the required pilgrimage for true disciples and "big" people.

> *"In the beginning God created the heavens and the earth."*
>
> (Genesis 1:1)

All the Trinity were active together in this magnificent event.

> *"Now the earth was formless and empty, darkness was over the surface of the deep, and the Spirit of God was hovering over the waters. And God said . . . "*   (Genesis 1:2–3)

The power of God's Word and Spirit consorting as they did in the creation is often repeated throughout Scripture. We will take a journey through three other incidents.

In the middle of a strong prophetic flow concerning the surrounding nations, Ezekiel confesses,

> *"The hand of the LORD was upon me."*   (Ezekiel 37:1)

He was brought by the Spirit to the middle of a valley full of bones. Having given him time to observe their number and dryness, the Lord then asked another of the Old Testament's great questions,

> *"Son of man, can these bones live?"*   (Ezekiel 37:3)

It's a faith question. The prophet admits that only the Lord knows. How liberating to enjoy the freedom of not knowing and being able to admit it! I wish more Christian leaders and politicians would practise such humility. Among the wider implications of the prophecy, two distinct instructions are conveyed to the prophet. First,

> "*Prophesy to these bones and say to them, 'Dry bones, hear the word of the Lord!'*"   (Ezekiel 37:4)

Second,

> "*Prophecy to the breath, 'Come . . . O breath . . . that they may live.'*"
> (Ezekiel 37:9)

This is the same conspiracy that worked in the Genesis creation: the Word and the Spirit. It is important to remember what happened in the valley of dry bones. Life did not immediately come with the prophesied word, but there was a big shake-up. In my experience, that is fairy normal! Whether the Word of the Lord comes to an individual, a family, a church, a denomination or a nation, change, disturbance and previously unwelcomed activity follow. The most basic word to describe such events is repentance: a change of mind and heart. Then the breath of the Spirit comes and a valley full of lifeless corpses becomes a vast army (Ezekiel 37:10).

Now we move Testaments and look in on the events surrounding the birth of Jesus. Luke relates to us that Mary, a favoured person, will have a son who will be called Jesus (Luke 1:30–32). Mary's question, *"How will this be, since I am a virgin?"* is very reasonable. Hold your breath in awe and wonder as events beyond full human understanding are described.

> "*The Holy Spirit will come upon you, and the power of the Most High will overshadow you. So the Holy One to be born will be called the Son of God.*"   (Luke 1:35)

My belief is that the same "conspiracy", the Word in the form of a seed carried by the Holy Spirit and placed within the virgin womb, produced a creative miracle, the Holy One – for nothing is impossible with God. The original Hebrew word *dabar* may be translated equally "word" or "thing". Only the context determines which English word is used. What an interesting thought! Can we conclude that for God every *word* is already a *thing* (even if we cannot see it yet) and therefore every–*thing* was previously a *word*? Paul seems to say something similar of the Word of God:

> *"For by Him all things were created . . . all things were created by Him and for Him. He is before all things, and in Him all things hold together."*   (Colossians 1:16–17)

Furthermore, Hebrews 1:3 speaks of the Son, *"Sustaining all things by His powerful word."* So if He can say it, it will be. No word, no thing is impossible with God!

Now here is a final illustration of this creative power, released when the Word and the Spirit conspire. Peter, writing in his first epistle says,

> *"You have been born again, not of perishable seed, but of imperishable, through the living and enduring word of God."*   (1 Peter 1:23)

"Born again" has become a catch phrase for those within evangelical Christianity, or for a perceived moral and political stance, the latter view generally being somewhat flawed and inaccurate. The words of Jesus in John 3 to a deeply religious, pious man, Nicodemus, may still ring with uncomfortable tones to the many similar, deeply religious, pious, Christianised people of Western civilisation. The biblical facts are inescapable: being a Christian does not happen through mental assent (helpful though an understanding of our faith is), nor through any religious ceremony, however well-intentioned. It only happens when the nature of God, His genetic make-up if you can accept such an idea, His imperishable seed, His Word, is placed within us, by the Holy Spirit. John's first epistle says,

> *"No one who is born of God will continue to sin, because God's seed remains in him; he cannot go on sinning, because he has been born of God."* (1 John 3:9)

The original word for seed is *sperma*. God's *sperma* – the seed of His nature and life placed within us! Paul puts the concept this way:

> *"Therefore, if anyone is in Christ, he is a new creation; the old has gone, the new has come!"* (2 Corinthians 5:17)

Being born again, becoming a Christian, is therefore a miracle. The same Word and Spirit that made the world out of nothing, turned a valley of dry bones into a standing army, and co-operated in the wonderful virgin birth of Jesus the Son of God, can also bring my life back to God's original "Garden of Eden" intentions, as soon as I realise my sinfulness and turn in repentance, confessing Jesus as Lord.

For me this miracle took place in Belfast, Northern Ireland in 1953. One September Sunday afternoon, Mrs Martin, my faithful Sunday School teacher, helped me, with many tears, to pray the sinner's prayer, "Lord, be merciful to me, a sinner." Sure, it was a ten year old boy's decision; granted, I had been brought up in a Christian culture. However, I'm a "big boy" now. I've looked at life, its religions and philosophies, enjoyed the privilege of travelling widely, and my decision is as resolute as ever. I would want the miracle of new birth, forgiveness, peace with God, being joined again to His eternal plan and purpose, today, if I had delayed so long in deciding.

If, as you read, you are conscious of the strange but compelling overtures of God's Spirit urging you to repentance and new birth, however religious or pagan you have been, stop now, pray, and ask God to forgive you. Thank Him that Christ's blood, poured out at the cross, paid for your and every man's sin. Ask Him to take charge of your life and invite Him to come and live in and with you, and to give you eternal life.

This miracle and the ongoing work of the Word and the Spirit are necessary for the making of "big" people, disciples of Jesus with the potential to turn the world upside down! What a tragedy that the Evangelical and Charismatic branches of the Church have historically been nervous of one another, not good at listening to each other, and subsequently weaker because they both need each other's message. Thank God that in recent years things have been better, but there is much room for progress. It has long been said that if all we had was the *Word*, we would *dry up*; if all we had was the *Spirit*, we would *blow up*; but that if we had an equal measure of both we would *grow up*. A balance of the Word and the Spirit is what releases God's creative power and brings us to new birth and maturity.

For the remainder of this chapter I want to concentrate on a plot that keeps most Christians immature. If you accept my premise that the Word and the Spirit working together release the secret of creation, then what must an opposing power do to prevent this from happening? Simply neutralise one or both of the components and the miracle cannot happen. Let us focus on the Word dimension first.

The recorded opening remarks of the speaking serpent, man's enemy, are to question whether God has really spoken: *"Did God really say . . . ?"* (Genesis 3:1). He always questions, always undermines God's Word. Many people do not believe that the Bible is God's Word, and therefore do not accept its living power to speak into and to direct their lives. Only when we accept that the Bible is the Word of God will its power properly work in us.

Christians firmly know and accept that the Bible is the Word of God, so how is its power neutralised? When you read the

Bible do any of the following things ever happen: your mind wanders and you find it very difficult to concentrate; you remember things that you have forgotten to do; you feel very tired and sleepy? Do the same things happen when you pray? How surprising! We must learn to overcome these attempts to prevent God's Word making maximum impact on our lives.

When your mind wanders, go back and re-read the scripture as often as necessary until you grasp the meaning. Write down the things you are reminded of: "Phone x . . . Speak to y . . ." When overcome by tiredness, change your position, read aloud and make sure you are awake!

How can we positively co-operate with the Word?

1. **Hear**. Make sure the above problems don't stop you hearing God's voice through the Scriptures.

   "Speak, LORD, for your servant is listening."   (1 Samuel 3:9)

2. **Hide**. When God speaks to you, make conscious decisions to remember and write something down.

   "Mary treasured up all these things and pondered them in her heart."
   (Luke 2:19)

3. **Hold**. Confess in speech and through prayer the things God has said to you.
4. **Honour**. Whatever the Word tells you to do, do it!

Of course, the Spirit of God is implicitly involved in all these activities, but how can we consciously cooperate with His creative power?

1. **Be filled**. Some call it the Baptism of the Spirit, others the infilling, some the renewing. The powerful injunction of Ephesians 5 is to, *"Be being filled with the Spirit."* I have

found great help in the consistent and disciplined use of speaking in tongues. *"He who speaks in a tongue edifies himself"* (1 Corinthians 14:4), that is, he builds himself up.

2. **Use**. It has been said that the answer to the misuse of the gifts of the Spirit is not disuse, but "right-use". In the New Testament Paul urges Timothy to, *"Fan into flame the gift of God, which is in you"* (2 Timothy 1:6). "Use it or lose it" seems an appropriate expression. I will say more about the gifts of the Spirit in the next two chapters.

3. **Develop**. Respond to the challenge of increasing the areas of your ministry. Enlarge your faith circle. When was the last time you did something for the first time?

4. **Honour**. As with the Word of God, the Spirit of God must be honoured and urgently obeyed. This requires a gentle sensitivity to His kind urgings.

This principle of the creative power of the Word and the Spirit combining is illustrated in the diagram below.

Cooperating with the Word and the Spirit of God as I have encouraged you to will feed the miracle of new birth that is the Christian's inheritance. Revelation will unfold concepts of

the greatness of God. Obedience will make clearer the amazing plans God has for each of our lives. We shall grow to become the disciples Jesus can effectively use in the building of His Church. The secret of creation will be at work in us!

Live In the Spirit . . .
Look Out, World!

14

The Evangelical and Charismatic divide which I referred to in the previous chapter is further overcome if a proper understanding of life in the Spirit is grasped. The historic Holiness Movements have seen life in the Spirit encompassed in a death to the self-life (expressed by some in water baptism), replaced by living in union with Christ. Other Evangelicals emphasise the manifestation of the fruit of the Spirit. The Charismatics have majored on the baptism in the Spirit and the use of His gifts as their interpretation of life in the Spirit. I'm greedy, and want to live with the best of both worlds, dead to self and alive in Christ, producing spiritual fruit, living a Spirit-filled life and using His gifts. This is the normal Christian life – life in the Spirit.

The New Testament provides a stiff challenge, which I cannot fully meet until each of these aspects of living in the power of the Spirit are a vibrant reality in my daily experience. How can I claim, *"it is for freedom that Christ has set us free"* (Galatians 5:1), and that, *"those who are led by the Spirit of God are sons of God"* (Romans 8:14), if in my humanity, in my world of work, I am constantly overcome by temptation; if in the secrecy of my mind I am not free; and if in my relationships I fall short of God's best through anger, bitterness, lust or any other vile thing? Evangelicals are wary of undisciplined Charismatics who speak in tongues but fail to live in personal victory, and rightly so. Paul issued a caution regarding this matter:

> *"If I speak in the tongues of men and angels, but have not love, I am only a resounding gong or a clanging cymbal."*
>
> (1 Corinthians 13:1)

The victory of Christ comes as we understand and appropriate His death and resurrection. In Galatians 5 the fruit of the Spirit, the manifestation of God's personality, is sandwiched between a call to freedom (verse 13), a challenge to live by the Spirit (verse 16), a confession that the acts of the sinful nature prevent our inheriting the kingdom of God (verses 19–21), and a statement that those who belong to Christ Jesus have crucified the sinful nature.

Living by the Spirit will be evident through fruit: love, joy, peace, patience, kindness, goodness, faithfulness, gentleness and self control (verses 22–23). However, this is only after crucifixion, and you cannot crucify yourself. I must appropriate daily the fact that I died in Christ:

"In the same way, count yourselves dead to sin, but alive to God in Christ Jesus" (Romans 6:11), and that He will live out His resurrection life through me:

> *"I have been crucified with Christ and I no longer live, but Christ lives in me."*
>
> (Galatians 2:20)

Appropriating the full work of the cross of Jesus, as I most certainly do, probably qualifies me as a card-carrying Evangelical. Sin no longer reigns. This does not mean that I never sin, but that sin has no control in my life. Friends and family can see the fruit of a changed life. The Charismatics argue that Jesus promised,

> *"Anyone who has faith in me will do what I have been doing. He will do even greater things than these."*
>
> (John 14:12)

They rightly ask the Evangelical, "If you are truly living by the Spirit, where are the miracles, the works of Jesus, the fullness of the gifts?" Many Evangelicals have tried to prove a dispensational view, a first-century-only relevance for the pentecostal power of New Testament Christianity. Some argue from 1 Corinthians 13 that love is everything, that prophecy will cease, and the childish things will be put away, yet the thrust of this passage is the coming of perfection, when we see face to face. We have not reached that place yet! Surely the weight of Paul's argument is not for one option or the other, but for both.

> *"Follow the way of love and eagerly desire spiritual gifts, especially the gift of prophecy."*   (1 Corinthians 14:1)

God is not mean. All the people of God should embrace the two elements of life in the Spirit: a changed nature bearing fruit, and a changed life exhibiting power.

I have enjoyed a personal filling of Holy Spirit for almost fifty years. The early years of my experience were both blessed and unnecessarily restricted. A very limited interpretation of Paul's teaching about the distribution of the gifts of the Spirit left me with the idea that I could only experience and use *some* of the gifts. Today I believe differently. Clearly, Scripture teaches that different manifestations of the Spirit (1 Corinthians 12:7–11) are given to individual members of the Body of Christ. Step back from the outworking of the gift and think about the in-working. What happened when God in the person of Holy Spirit came to live in the tent of my humanity? As the Scripture says,

> *"Your body is a temple of the Holy Spirit."*   (1 Corinthians 6:19)

For me it was a glorious experience. What did I receive? It was a miracle, which I cannot fully express or comprehend; I received God's Spirit. It was not a fragment of Him, or a part of His personality or character, but God's Spirit.

All that is the nature of God can find an expression through the Spirit. Let me clarify the word "gifts". 1 Corinthians 12:31 tells us to, *"Eagerly desire the greater gifts."* We are often tempted to associate this with a tangible "present" given to us, but this is unhelpful in our understanding of the biblical word. It is *charisma*, meaning grace or favour, and is better interpreted as an outflowing or manifestation of God's nature; God's grace revealed through us. A firmer grasp of the fact that all of God's Spirit is available to express Himself through each of us using what are traditionally called the nine gifts of the Spirit will widen our horizons and the potential for God to work through us using the Spirit's power. I believe that each of the manifestations in the 1 Corinthians 12:7–11 list conveys a facet of God's nature. For instance, God is omniscient, He knows everything. A message of wisdom, a message of knowledge, and the ability to distinguish between spirits are therefore fragments of His all-knowingness. They are gifts to help our weakness of understanding and experience. They are God's omniscience working through our lives. To believe that all the gifts, the *charisma*, can find expression through my life is to give me a far greater potential.

> *"All these are the work of one and the same Spirit, and He gives them to each one, just as He determines."*   (1 Corinthians 12:11)

What happens in practice? I believe that according to the need of our ministry, in relation to our faith and, sometimes, personality, we develop a stronger ability in specific areas of gift. We have faith to operate with confidence in certain spiritual gifts because of previous experience. But God is not mean, for He longs to express more of Himself through you. This will include the miracle of a changed life and victory over sin, the miracle of a changed personality with fruit to prove it, and the miracle of God's indwelling Spirit expressing His personality and power through our humanity. Let's go for the whole package. Live in the Spirit – look out, world! These people are developing the character and drawing on the power that helped the early Christians turn their world upside down!

* * *

Anything more than the most casual reading of the New Testament will lead to several conclusions, one of which is that to be a part of the Body of Christ we must have a life changing, new birth experience. A second and equally clear conclusion is that to function as an active, vital part of the Body of Christ we need the same power that the first century Christians enjoyed; and thank God, it is *still* Pentecost! We could also say we need their boldness, commitment and faith. In earlier chapters I have talked about the anointed leaders as a team of Spirit-filled people in relationship, who are training and discipling the rest of the community, especially the next generation of leaders in the equivalent of the cathedral's cloisters. Do not conclude from my use of that word that I refer to some closed world, separated from the reality of daily life. If the training is to be credible and successful it will prove itself in the rough and tumble of life, fighting the good fight of faith, doing things for the first time and breaking through the present boundaries of our faith and experience. A disciple called Ananias had one of those faith-stretching experiences which we all know are good for us, but none of us want to go through. We read about it in Acts 9. A short study of the passage will help us better understand the practicalities of the teaching on the gifts of the Spirit covered earlier.

Ananias is a classic illustration of the outworking of gifts, just as the Spirit determines and as the situation demands. In verse 10 he responds to God calling to him in a vision. In verses 11–12 he is given information and direction. In verses 13–14 he quite understandably expresses concern about Saul's reputation. In verses 14–16 a sharp instruction is given, with more information. In verses 17–19 Ananias follows God's instructions implicitly, finds things as God had declared (how surprising!) and succeeds in his mission. The whole episode is quite a drama, a display of God's omniscience, omnipresence and omnipotence. The disciple is not mentioned again, but I am confident he continued serving the Master, filled with the Spirit.

God revealed Himself through the gifts of the Spirit operating in Ananias. Time has passed, but the opportunities are the same for Christ's disciples today.

Ananias used . . .

1. **Words of knowledge**. Several clear and specific pieces of information were given:

   "Go to the house of Judas on Strait Street and ask for a man of Tarsus named Saul, for he is praying."

2. **Words of wisdom**. The skill and ability to use the knowledge to advantage:

   "He has seen a man named Ananias come and place his hands on him to restore his sight."

3. **Faith**. With the command, *"Go!"* I believe Ananias received supernatural faith.
4. **Prophecy**. The statement, *"My chosen instrument to carry my name before the Gentiles and their kings"* was accepted by Paul and became part of his testimony and mandate.
5. **A Gift of healing**.

   "Jesus . . . has sent me so that you may see again."

There is no mention of the use of the gift of tongues in the narrative when Ananias prayed for Saul to, *"Be filled with the Holy Spirit,"* but it is clear that five of the nine gifts (even excluding speaking in tongues) mentioned in 1 Corinthians 12:7–10 found expression in the events of Saul's conversion. It is also true that there is no specific information to suggest that Ananias was anything other than a "normal" disciple. We can conclude that every twentieth century Christian has the same gifts available and that all are candidates for usefulness.

Any church seeking to live by the doctrine and practice of the New Testament should expect God's Spirit to use all of its members in various facets of its life. The gifts of revelation are essential in organisational and directional decisions, in difficult pastoral issues and in confronting sin. The gifts of supernatural power are needed in healing the sick and seeing people miraculously released. The gifts of presence bring encouragement, hope and comfort to the people of God. All this works in major and minor matters, in macro and micro issues. The whole community of believing people should live with an expectancy of the Spirit's involvement and "interference" at any time, on any issue, through anybody, for the glory of God and the establishment of His Kingdom. That sounds and feels like Church should be. Why then have we cultivated such a tame and insipid version of the Church in most of Western Christianity?

In many Evangelical churches there is little or no expectation of the supernatural in anything other than conversion. In many Charismatic churches a predictable spiritual song and occasional tongues, interpretation and prophecy are the limit of our expectations. A.W. Tozer declared,

> The Bible teaches us that the genuine gifts of the Holy Spirit are a necessity in the spiritual life and ministries of every Christian congregation serious about glorifying Jesus Christ as Saviour and Lord.[1]

Donald Gee, a notable early Pentecostal, wrote,

> They [the gifts] were to provide a spiritual capability far mightier than the finest natural abilities could ever supply; and, deeper

still, they were to provide the supernatural basis for a supernatural order of ministry.[2]

I will add one further poetic but powerful comment from
Harold Horton:

> Shall the Church of God be content with the metaphor in place
> of the might, the coloured windows and altar lamps instead of
> the omnipotent energies of the Holy Spirit? Shall we not by
> wondrous grace restore to the suffering world the healing
> instead of the haloed Christ, the mighty instead of the mitred
> apostles, the unctionised instead of the canonised messenger
> of the Gospel of complete redemption? The energies of the
> unchanging Spirit are still available for earth's desperate needs
> at the desire of the humble.[3]

What can we do to regain the momentum of supernatural
ministry? We must recognise that much disuse of the gifts of
the Spirit has resulted from extremism and misuse. We must
diligently follow the teaching of the New Testament, expecting
and being available to the Spirit. We would be greatly helped
by experienced people discipling and helping others to use the
gifts properly. As John Wimber expressed it,

> Anyone born again has the potential of experiencing the power
> and gifts of the Holy Spirit. We should expect this experience
> – Scripture teaches it is a part of the normal Christian life. If
> the experience of the Holy Spirit is not preached or seen by
> Christians . . . they will not expect these things to happen, and
> they will not happen.[4]

We therefore require a very different approach to the use of
gifts than that employed by many Charismatics. Further, we
must learn to develop a greater openness, and develop a greater
openness to learn.

We must have a new love for the Holy Spirit as a Person, companion, comforter and guide, and train ourselves to seek God's face and to "be being filled" with the Spirit. We should let the Holy Spirit use us in any way, however great or small, as He develops our sensitivity to His prompting and will. As we seek Him our desire shall be not self-projection but service, using gifts *"for the strengthening of the church"* (1 Corinthians 14:26).

Notes

1. Tozer, A.W., *Tragedy in the Church: The Missing Gifts.* Christian Publications Inc., 1976.

2. Gee, D., *Concerning Spiritual Gifts.* Gospel Publishing House, Springfield, MO, 1980, p. 26.

3. Horton, H., *The Gifts of the Spirit,* (10th ed.). Evangel Press, 1974, p. 29.

4. Wimber, J., *Power Evangelism; Signs and Wonders Today.* Hodder and Stoughton, 1985, p. 142.

SECTION 4
The Unstoppable Church

The Outworking

If You Don't Belong, You Can't Stay

15

The intensive work of preparation that has been continuing in the cloisters should be taking "called" people, refining their characters and sharpening their appreciation of the power of the Word of God and their operational understanding of the ministry of Holy Spirit. With senior leaders, opportunities for service within the Cathedral life or its associated ministries will further mature each gift. This life is *"the fullness of Him"* (Ephesians 1:23) that will *"prepare God's people for works of service"* (Ephesians 4:12) as they *"become mature, attaining to the whole measure of the fullness of Christ"* (Ephesians 4:13). In the remaining chapters of this book we will look at the inward life of the Body of Christ, and also at the dramatic and radical ministry that is the outward life, as *"each part does its work"* (Ephesians 4:16). Producing the quality of people required will, I suggest, result in an explosion of ministry that is nothing less than God's people being the hands and feet of Jesus in every area where His love is needed, releasing a pent-up flood of devotion, enthusiasm and desire for Him, and representing Jesus to the world. First though, let us look at that which I have called the internal life of church.

The human body, full of life but with no skeleton, no support structure, would be an awful heap of uncontrollable flesh. Conversely, a perfectly formed skeleton with every part of the human anatomy in place, but without life, is a corpse. Developing the illustration, different cells reproduce consistently inside the human body and our continuing life depends on this process. When the cellular reproduction programme becomes uncontrolled we call it cancer. This "rogue life" threatens life itself.

Many years ago my brother Andrew began travelling extensively in many parts of the world. He would often return with observations about the content and style of the churches he had visited. Many of them were high on outward style and organisation but weak on spiritual life. Others were full of faith and life, throbbing with spiritual energy, but badly organised and therefore less efficient and less successful than they could be. Few were high-scoring on organisation and structure as well as on vital spiritual life. How sad! How do we provide enough skeletal organisation to support the vital life which keeps the Body of Christ fully operational? There must be a definite structure. The human body only works properly as it receives instruction from the head through the nervous system. In the same way, Christ is the Head of the Church and has delegated responsibility to leaders for the proper direction of the work of the Church. Part of the authority structure in the human body is the immune system: the body has a built-in ability to either accept or reject that which it does not recognise as being of itself. The Body of Christ needs this ability also.

We say at my home church in Nottingham, "If you don't belong you can't stay, and if you do belong you can't leave." It is important that we strike the right balance in people belonging, that they should claim personal membership of the church to which they belong. Part of me knows that whoever, with integrity, can share the bread with me in Communion is my brother; we already belong to the "one Body", the Universal Church. Nonetheless, another part of me knows that some clear criteria and an expected level of commitment and behaviour also help people and leaders alike to identify those belonging to any specific part of the Body of Christ, namely the local church. In the past I have tended to accept those who offer their hand in fellowship, while some of my friends have put more emphasis upon the need for commitment. The truth, as usual, involves a dynamic tension holding both positions. I have found it difficult to understand why very experienced Christians must go through a complete commitment programme, including some basic teaching which is necessary for young Christians, before being fully accepted into a new fellowship. On the other hand, it must be right that all new people come to an understanding of the vision and philosophy of the church group they are being joined to. Without some form of membership, including recognising the leaders and understanding the active place of each member, I believe that the skeleton will not support the expected life of the body adequately. Once again, a dynamic balance must be obtained to allow the normal life and growth of the body.

Speaking as a non-conformist Christian, the formal life of a physical cathedral is to me simultaneously a fascination, a mystery and a frustration: in fact, a whole host of emotions! I have enjoyed sitting in the choir stalls and worshipping during evensong, but I could not sit there every day! Many times in the past, I have enjoyed using some of the great and ancient prayers of the Anglican Prayer Book, but I would freeze if the formal service and offices were all I could use for prayer and praise. The many links with all that has gone before, the present communion of saints, and the maintaining of the Christian calendar all provide a sense of stability and permanence that many of us could and should learn from.

We must remind ourselves that the internal life of the church, to ensure its health, must include reproduction. It is a basic truth that all healthy things grow. It is also true that the continuance of the human family is dependent on reproduction. These natural facts are applicable to the spiritual family, the Body of Christ. After a dew days ministry in Northern Europe on one occasion, Monday morning found me catching up with many things in the life of our own fellowship. What a joy and delight for me to learn that in both the evening meetings the previous day, people had been baptised and had given excellent testimonies showing evidence of truly changed lives; furthermore, six people had responded to the Good News of Jesus! Nothing is more exciting in the normal daily life of church than conversion growth, where family, friends, neighbours, work mates, anybody, everybody can come and find that which we have found: peace with God, forgiveness, and a new sense of purpose for living. The arrival of a baby into a loving home brings new challenges, new responsibilities, and necessary changes of routine, but it is all exciting nevertheless. Similarly, the internal life and health of church is radically challenged by the advent of new birth. All our organisation, structure and hard work become meaningful and worthwhile, and change occurs as necessary to "get the job done".

* * *

We are now in the Nave, the main body of the Cathedral, and our thinking is focused on the main acts of worship, prayer and teaching that make up the daily life of most cathedrals. Thinking first about worship, I was reading again the remarkable words of Isaiah 30. This chapter is in the middle of the multiple woes breathed out against many nations. The heading in my Bible is, "Woe to the Obstinate Nation". In the midst of the judgement of God, the second half of the chapter reveals the kindness and compassion of the sovereign Lord:

> *"In repentance and rest is your salvation,*
>   *in quietness and trust is your strength"*   (Isaiah 30:15)

and,

> *" . . . yet the* Lord *longs to be gracious to you;*
>   *he rises to show you compassion."*   (Isaiah 30:18)

The chapter changes tempo from verse 27 onwards revealing God in His power, using the praises of His people as an accompaniment to the punishment of their enemies. There are many powerful statements, for example, *"His tongue is a consuming fire"* (verse 27), *"He shakes the nations in the sieve of destruction"* (verse 28) and, *"The voice of the Lord will shatter Assyria"* (verse 31). Sandwiched between these comments, we are shown the people of God celebrating in praise:

> *"And you will sing*
> *   as on the night you celebrate a holy festival;*
> *your hearts will rejoice*
> *   as when people go up with flutes*
> *to the mountain of the Lord,*
> *   to the Rock of Israel."*   (Isaiah 30:29)

God is next shown to be striking the Assyrian enemy to the rhythm of the music of the people of God:

> *"Every stroke the Lord lays on them*
> *   with his punishing rod*
> *will be to the music of tambourines and harps,*
> *   as he fights them in battle with the blows of his arm."*
>   (Isaiah 30:32)

What a picture!

Three times every year the people of God had their major festivals and many went on pilgrimage to the temple, the house of the Lord. Psalm 89:15 says,

> *"Blessed are those who have learned to acclaim you."*

Other translations of the same passage speak of the joyful sound, the festal shout, as a noise of acclamation. These are the songs to which Isaiah is referring when the people of God shouted and sang with great joy and rejoicing on their way to the temple. Psalms 120–134, the Songs of Ascent, take on new meaning when understood as being the songs which were sung when going to the temple. Some scholars say that they were used on the journey, others say that they were sung upon approaching the holy buildings. Whatever is true, the people of God were blessed as they released their emotions of joy and thankfulness in playing, singing, dancing and shouting.

Back to Isaiah 30 for a moment. What a revelation to understand that during their praise and rejoicing the Lord was striking their enemies to the beat of tambourines and harps! That is by no means the whole picture for the passage concludes with a graphic description of Topheth as a place of fire and burning (Isaiah 30:33). This place, by whatever name, can be traced in the Old Testament to the place where children were sacrificed in the fires of worship to the detestable god Molech, and became identified with the place for burning rubbish outside Jerusalem. The Bible uses it as a picture of hell, the place of torment prepared for the devil and all his angels (see Revelation 20:10; 2 Peter 2:4). Would it be outrageous to conclude that not only does God punish enemies during our praise, but that the demonic kingdom is made aware of its future home and can maybe even smell the sulphurous burning of that dreadful place as the incense of thankful praise and worship ascend to the throne of God? It is at least an exciting thought!

God delights in the praises of His people (Psalm 147:11). The password into His presence is "Thank You" (Psalm 100, *The Message*). Praise and worship are powerful. The essence of our humanity, made in God's image and likeness, was created for worship. The Scriptures portray the Father as searching for, seeking out, and looking diligently . . . for what? For worshippers.

> *"The true worshippers will worship the Father in Spirit and truth, for they are the kind of worshippers the Father seeks. God is Spirit, and His worshippers must worship in spirit and in truth."*   (John 4:23–24)

In many congregations there is the danger of exchanging the hymn board or traditional "hymn sandwich", I think they call it, for what can be aptly described as a "powerpoint marathon": service after service of repeating the formula, with a different formula in each of the various denominational streams. Please, please let us again recover worship in Spirit and in truth, with everything done decently and in order, but never resisting the pull of the Spirit to move in the direction He chooses (John 4:24; Isaiah 43:19)!

It is important that we widen our thinking about worship. What exactly is it? The word means, among other things, to bow toward, to pay obeisance or homage. Looking around a cathedral may provide some clues to its wider meaning. The construction of the building required a huge sacrifice of time and financial resources for the glory of God. Many of the windows attempt to focus our thoughts on His surpassing glory. The table reminds us of Christ's sacrifice. I am not for a moment suggesting that we should again build such places, or fill our buildings with altars, lamps and coloured glass, but I am strongly recommending that the living stones, we who are the people of God, who are this Cathedral, should display in our lives a commitment similar to that of those ancient builders and should live daily with an understanding of the surpassing glory of God, presenting our bodies as living sacrifices. We are told that this is our reasonable service or spiritual worship in response to Christ's once-and-for-all act of submission, namely, His death on the cross (Romans 12:1–2). The daily ritual of morning and evening worship may have become a routine for many in the life of the world's cathedrals, but I am sure that they were intended, at least in part, to be focal points in time and consciousness when praise and thanks were rendered to God for His great goodness and grace, and the worshippers reminded themselves of their complete dependence on Him for life and breath. Somehow, through services or whatever mechanism helps us, we the living stones must, through our words, thoughts, actions, and in the totality of our lives render ourselves in worship to God. It has been said many times that worship is a lifestyle; it is more than words and actions, it is our life. Everything about us, including our words and actions, must emanate perfume, bringing glory to God. Perhaps such a group of people meeting together will become a *"Holy temple in the Lord, built together to become a dwelling in which God lives by His Spirit"* (Ephesians 2:21–22).

The effect would be that,

> *"The manifold wisdom of God should be made known to the rulers and authorities in the heavenly realms."*   (Ephesians 3:10)

Our services will then know a fresh vitality, with everything done decently and in order (1 Corinthians 14:40), and, like the many instruments of an orchestra playing beautiful music with great skill under the baton of a inspired conductor, together we will make music and worship in Spirit and in truth.

Supplementary effects of such worship will be a happy, voluntary devotion to doing God's will as we live our lives to please Him, working hard, having personal and corporate integrity, and enjoying the blessing of giving more than receiving. In private and public, our lives should be worship. People are attracted to this kind of worshipper.

Thinking about style and structure in our worship services, we need the breath of the Spirit and divine creativity to balance the necessary routines, the accepted "rites of passage" that help us to feel secure, with the spontaneous openness which allows the Holy Spirit to lead us in new ways into all truth, without hype or triviality, always helping people onward in their pilgrimage as worshippers. There are a huge variety of styles and emphases to be found in worship in different cultures of the world. Rightly or wrongly, the culture of the people does find expression in their worship; sometimes it is too strong and on other occasions it may be too weak. I find it difficult to endorse or understand the adoption or enforcement of the music and worship style typical to the Western hemisphere upon the people of a very different culture and mindset with whom I have enjoyed worshipping God. We are in danger of repeating the mistake made by some well-intentioned but misled missionaries to tropical lands, of imposing incongruous Western architecture and three-piece suits for Sunday worship on the people whom they served.

More than thirty years ago my lifelong Pentecostal worship habits were severely shaken by a new understanding from the Holy Spirit. I am sure that part of the momentum for the release of praise and worship so evident around the world during the past couple of decades is a Holy Spirit inspired orchestration of a global Hallelujah chorus. Remember what the great crowd shouted in the historic enactment of the prophetic writing in Zechariah 9:9?

> *"Hosanna!*
> *Blessed is He who comes in the name of the Lord!*
> *Blessed is the King of Israel!"*   (John 12:13)

Thinking further back in time, after the prophetic poetry of suffering in Psalm 22, and the great picture of the Lord as my shepherd in Psalm 23, we come to the majestic overture, *"The earth is the LORD's,"* followed by the powerful insight of the ancient doors being opened to let the King of Glory come in. Whether these doors are the long closed East gate of the city of Jerusalem, or the portals of heaven, or both, I do not know, but my spirit rejoices that the ancient pictures of the Old Testament, the actual events of the life of Jesus, and the declared coronation of the King of kings are being echoed in the present explosion of Hosannas around the world and in heaven. This concept makes our praise part of something much bigger, grander and more splendid than anything we can contemplate in this temporal realm. It does, of course, make a nonsense of

any of us claiming a current copyright to total understanding
of the working of the Spirit in worship. The great orchestras
in the huge Korean churches, the repeating rhythms of African
singing to the beat of home-made percussion, the haunting
minor keys of Eastern Europe, the flags and hymn singing of
North America, the unique and specific styles of many new
churches, the plainsong chanting of the Psalms – all are part of
this shout of praise. Oh for a thousands tongues, and even a
thousand styles in which to sing!

Before we conclude these thoughts on the worship life of the
people of God, and turn to the dynamic place of prayer in
the Cathedral of living stones, let us take a brief look at those
psalms, the Songs of Ascent I mentioned earlier. Does it help
you worship if you know that when you call in distress, He
answers (Psalm 120:1); that your help comes from the Lord
(Psalm 121:2); that you can go to the house of the Lord (Psalm
122:1); that God's throne is in heaven (Psalm 123:1); that the Lord
has been on our side (Psalm 124:2); that the Lord surrounds His
people (Psalm 125:2); that our mouths are filled with laughter
because the Lord has done great things for us (Psalm 126:2–3);
that the Lord builds the house and sons are a heritage from the
Lord (Psalm 127:1–3); that a man is blessed who fears the Lord
(Psalm 128:4); that the Lord has cut me free from the chords of
the wicked (Psalm 129:4); that with the Lord there is forgiveness
(Psalm 130:4); that your hope is in the Lord (Psalm 131:3); that
the Lord has clothed you with salvation (Psalm 132:16); and
that the Lord bestows His blessings (Psalm 133:3)? If it does,
and it should, then,

> "Praise the LORD, all you servants of the LORD
>   who minister by night in the house of the LORD.
> Lift up your hands in the sanctuary
>   and praisethe LORD.
> May the LORD, the Maker of heaven and earth,
>   bless you from Zion."   (Psalm 134)

A House of Prayer
or a Den of Thieves?

Early in His public ministry, close to the time of the Passover feast, Jesus made His way to Jerusalem. The temple area was full of corrupt commercial activity, the buying and selling of animals and the exchanging of money. Indignant at the extortion and manipulation, Jesus overturned the money changers' tables.

> *"To those who sold doves He said, 'Get these out of here! How dare you turn my Father's house into a market!'"* (John 2:16)

A somewhat different picture from the "gentle Jesus, meek and mild" character of modern invention! But, avoiding implications of corruption, are we any better, with a mass of activities in and around the life of many churches, buying and selling, people using the time of fellowship to do business? This may be perfectly valid in its right place, but is it what Father's house is for? Through Isaiah, God describes His house as, *"My house of prayer"* (Isaiah 56:7). Later in the same verse God states, *"My house will be called a house of prayer for all nations."* Thus, in dedicated buildings, and in the homes, offices, and hearts of the people, the Cathedral should be a twenty-four-hours-a-day house of prayer, validating the New Testament principle that each believer is a temple of the Holy Spirit (1 Corinthians 6:19). The presence of God is not confined to a physical temple.

Many books have been written about prayer. Prayer diaries and notes are to be found everywhere, but I am not sure how many people actually pray. Let me say immediately that I rejoice at the upsurge of energy and enthusiasm for prayer in recent years. Many leaders in the field of church growth have been made aware that prayer is one of the most powerful weapons available to them, and have bravely advanced the frontiers of understanding to include spiritual warfare and intercession, among other issues, which have in the past been considered "fringe" matters.

I grew up in a preacher's house, my father being a full-time pastor from the time I was two-and-a-half years old. I often heard him pray and saw first-hand answers to his and my mother's prayers as they lived devotional and prayerful lives. I know that prayer is real and I know that it works, but after all these years it is still a daily discipline to pray. I know that duty and discipline bring us to delight; I have read and experienced it too, but prayer is often work, nonetheless.

More than thirty years ago I began praying early in the morning with a handful of others, several days a week. Weeks of prayer with fasting were a part of our stronger emphasis. We learned a lot, we grew in our spiritual life, and the church grew too. In the late 1970s I had become very burdened when reading the book of the prophet Joel, and God brought a man to join me who had received the same burden from the same chapters. John and I began to pray through each Friday night. Sometimes we would succeed, somehow knowing that we'd broken through and had received new revelation and holy encouragement. Sometimes it was very hard work, we would become heavy and fall asleep, but we always pressed on. Without advertising, others began to come and pray with us. Over the years people have come and gone, and numbers have varied between a handful and a roomful. John joined me in full-time ministry, and over the years developed a prayer strategy including a "House of Prayer for All Nations" before being released to plant and lead his own church. In comparison with some of the great prayer programmes – the prayer mountains of Korea, the prayer houses of Argentina, the ceaseless intercession of many unsung heroes of the Gospel – the programme was very small, but it was a start. Today, a constant flow of prayer takes place in our InSpire Prayer Room and hundreds of hours of prayer take place every week as groups of prayer warriors *"Give Him* [the Lord] *no rest"* (Isaiah 62:6–7), and call on His name.

Alongside InSpire is a programme of intercession headed by women who watch over the gates of the city. They meet to pray in prayer camps across the city, for prayer breakfasts, and also to determine strategy. There are also prayer cells which regularly meet in some of the oldest church buildings of the city, and task forces with a brief to pray concerning specific areas in the life of the city. People from many other churches are joining in this programme of watching in prayer and intercession over the seven main pillars of our society: law and order, commerce, education, health and social services, media, politics and religion. In all these prayer strategies we are seeking . . .

> *"The peace and prosperity of the city to which I have carried you into exile. Pray to the LORD for it, because if it prospers, you too will prosper."* (Jeremiah 29:7)

God promises that as people return in repentance to Him, He *"will forgive all their sins of rebellion against me"* (Jeremiah 33:8), and He makes a further statement that we consistently confess over our own city of Nottingham:

> *"Then this city will bring me renown, joy, praise and honour before all nations on earth that hear of all the good things I do for it; and they will be in awe and will tremble at the abundant prosperity and peace I provide for it."* (Jeremiah 33:9)

During this period our church has continued to grow. All thanks and praise go to God. I am confident that believing prayer is responsible for the growth in no small part.

Let us think further about the difference between a House of Prayer and a Den of Thieves; phrased differently, "A house of giving or a place of getting." The Bible infers strong things about those whose prayers are self-centred, who have a "what-can-I-get-out-of-it" mentality. Recall what Jesus said about the Pharisee and the tax collector (Luke 18:9–14), or reflect upon the words of the Psalmist:

> *"If I had cherished sin in my heart,*
> *   the Lord would not have listened;*
> *but God has surely listened*
> *   and heard my voice in prayer."*   (Psalm 66:18–19)

The importance of prayer has been highlighted by Tennyson, one of our own poets:

> More things are wrought by prayer
> Than this world dreams of. Wherefore, let thy voice
> Rise like a fountain for me night and day.
> For what are men better than sheep or goats
> That nourish a blind life within the brain,
> If, knowing God, they lift not hands of prayer
> Both for themselves and those who call them friend?[1]

Part of the success of any Cathedral of living stones is to imbibe and practice the principle quoted in the words of Jesus,

> *"It is more blessed to give than to receive."*   (Acts 20:35)

An understanding of this is very important to successfully grasping the secrets of prayer. It would be helpful if the whole philosophy of the Church was built around giving first. The rich generosity of the Macedonian churches as recorded in 2 Corinthians 8–9 began with them giving *"themselves first to the Lord"*. This attitude releases finances (remember, there is no recession in the Kingdom of God!) and personnel, beginning with leaders being given to other needy ministries. Every church should try to give its leaders away to another ministry, preferably overseas, for some weeks of every year – and sponsor them going. Every part of the ministry will be blessed by this philosophy of giving. The Lord encouraged me years ago from the story in Genesis 15, with regards to my own "going out". God took Abram outside his tent and showed him the stars. How many times on overseas journeys serving the Lord have I stepped out from the tent of my own work and, suddenly, the stars! – resulting in a fresh understanding of the plan and purpose of God in my own life, family and church ministry.

A giving attitude further releases prayer and again this needs to start with the leaders. It speaks of a commitment to the needs and wellbeing of others. I am not suggesting for a moment that anyone neglect the personal devotional life of prayer, since we must all heed the injunction of Scripture:

> *"Pray in the Spirit on all occasions with all kinds of prayers and requests. With this in mind, be alert and always keep on praying for all the saints."*   (Ephesians 6:18)

The daily round of prayer in the ancient cathedral contained some of this other-centredness and we should learn from it. It will make us bigger, more caring and compassionate people. I have not met anyone who, after praying using a map or an atlas and any other helpful tools or information about the world, has not become a bigger and less self-centred person and consequently more aware of the needs of a dying world.

If our experience of authority is that it is delegated to the Church by its Head, Jesus Christ, then prayer is one of the areas that will most benefit from this insight. Part of the message of grace in Ephesians 2 involves us being *"Raised . . . up with Christ and seated . . . with Him in the heavenly realms in Christ Jesus"* (Ephesians 2:6).

If *"the Spirit helps us in our weakness"* and because *"we do not know what we ought to pray for, but the Spirit Himself intercedes for us"* (Romans 8:26–27), then in our position, with the Spirit's help, we understand that . . .

> *"Because Jesus lives forever, He has a permanent priesthood. Therefore He is able to save completely those who come to God through Him, because He always lives to intercede for them."*
>
> (Hebrews 7:24–25)

Could this mean that learning to listen to God, by the help of the Spirit, we will hear what Jesus is praying as He *"always lives to intercede"*, and that successful prayer is to join in agreement with Him? Maybe then the words of the Gospel will be more powerfully demonstrated. By virtue of the fact that we are seated with Him in heavenly places (Ephesians 2:6), we can be confident that the heavenly authority which we have received will be enforced in earthly situations. This is using our delegated authority. The Church has the opportunity and the potential of rising to properly represent Christ's power in the earth, and being the head instead of the tail, as is so often the case. These truths about our power in the unseen world must be understood clearly and used wisely. There is no place here for "gung-ho" adventurers peddling self-interest, but there is much room for sincere, godly, selfless intercessors who insist on the rule and domain of Christ being made more visible in our time and generation.

Watching many churches pass through repeated difficulties due to a painful split or a serious moral problem – to suggest only two situations – brings into sharper focus the scripture,

"Our struggle is not against flesh and blood, but against the rulers, against the authorities, against the powers of this dark world and against the spiritual forces of evil in the heavenly realms."

(Ephesians 6:12)

My observation of church problems over many years leads me to an unhappy but inevitable conclusion that many leaders and congregations have not fully grasped the unseen dimension of our warfare. A very different approach to solving problems would be evident if these principles were more clearly understood. There would be much less conflict amongst the flesh and blood!

It is enlightening and helpful to know that all anointed people are attacked. The illustration of King David helps to clarify this truth:

"When the Philistines heard that David had been anointed king of Israel, they went up in full force to search for him, but David heard about it and went down to the stronghold."   (2 Samuel 5:17)

Interesting! David then inquires of the Lord, a wise thing to do. The Philistines make the valley of Rephaim their place of conflict (some say a legitimate meaning of this name is, "the place of giants"). Our enemies will always try to choose their strong ground, which is usually our place of vulnerability. Thankfully, David had learned to deal with giants and so must we. David called the place Baal Perazim, the place where God breaks through. As we pray we must learn how to turn the place of giants and vulnerability, even potential defeat, into the place of glorious victory, the place of breakthrough and triumph. The Philistines regroup for a second attack and again David listens for the clear direction of God. How often we blunder on after a victory, thinking we have the answer, the right method, only to be reminded that we should have enquired of the Lord again! David obeys God's new direction and obtains the victory.

Did someone say that the devil only tempts us to fail, but the Lord tests us to succeed? Without a proper understanding of prayer, warfare and intercession, we will not achieve the level of breakthrough that we need in order to win the full victory God has prepared for us.

Life is a pilgrimage and prayer is part of that journey. We keep learning, journeying, making mistakes and enjoying breakthroughs, but we must never individually or corporately give up.

> *"Jesus told His disciples . . . that they should always pray and not give up."* (Luke 18:1)

The same principle applies to us.

I have learned a lot over the years from those whose main understanding of prayer is meditation, quietness or even the monastic life. In my youthful arrogance I was very surprised at how much I learned from spending time with Spirit-filled monks, even to the point of singing with them during a service on one occasion! I have, however, become more intolerant of ecumenical meetings whose prayer focus is only ever contemplative and formally structured. When they have learned to pass a noisy day in prayer, I will join in some of their quiet days! Much of Western Christianity appears to lack the fervour and intensity shown by the renewed Church in the developing world. How would Jesus, of whom the book of Hebrews records, *"He offered up prayers and petitions with loud cries and tears"* (Hebrews 5:7), respond to the cerebral structure of Western prayer? The writer to the Hebrews continues by asserting that Jesus' prayers were acceptable and successful.

> *"He was heard because of His reverent submission."*
> (Hebrews 5:7)

As with most things, I am not suggesting an either/or option here. Many noisy Charismatics would benefit greatly from times of quiet mediation and even structure in prayer. Conversely, many of my "quiet" brothers and sisters would be greatly blessed by learning a free and expressive abandonment to God's Spirit in prayer.

The emphasis which Western thinking places on the individual has brought into the arena of prayer a sense of personal responsibility and a desire to express, by whatever means, individual prayers and the prayers of individuals. This responsibility is both laudable and important. It does, however, leave us limited in our ability to express ourselves corporately. Beyond the responsive prayers of a formal liturgy and the declaring of Psalms, our experience is very weak.

In the developing world, where corporeity and the extended family are often significant factors in the normal lifestyle, I have enjoyed joining with hundreds – sometimes thousands – of people, all of us praying aloud together with great energy, emotion, enthusiasm and excitement. Acts 4:24 tells us that the early church *"raised their voices together in prayer to God."* The image is powerful. Some friends of mine were present at a public prayer rally in Seoul, Korea, where one million Christians prayed together. They found the experience hard to describe. I can hear the quintessentially English voice saying, "But we are not like that." If the Bible shows people praying aloud together, and if Jesus is heard praying with loud cries, then maybe we, in this instance, should step beyond our cultural boundaries and be like Jesus. I am sure that the prayer life of every Cathedral of living stones in the Western world would be enhanced by more corporate prayer. It is also true that in those societies where praying aloud together is already a regularly exercised discipline, the practice of individual prayer would be beneficial. Allow me to express myself about one further matter before leaving the house of prayer. Men are allowed, by the conventions of Western behaviour, to shout and express emotions in a limited number of contexts, sport being the most obvious example. Christian meetings most definitely do not come within this accepted remit. The Bible however, says, *"shout aloud and sing for joy"* (Isaiah 12:6), and we are further urged to *"clap your hands all you nations, shout to God with cries of joy"* (Psalm 47:1).

What a powerful release has come on the many occasions I have encouraged people, especially men, to break through the emotion barrier, the limitation of self-consciousness, and shout. Break that sound barrier! Perhaps with Joshua we should,

> *"Shout! For the Lord has given you the city!"*   (Joshua 6:16)

The foundations and authority structure of the Cathedral of living stones are established. The team of leaders is working well, developing other teams and supporting the vision. This experienced and anointed group are training and maturing the next generation of leaders and together they are enjoying the daily life of church, a lifestyle of worship, and, twenty-four-hours-a-day, the body prays. Now, how relevant are we making the teaching of truth so that the whole body, the complete building of living stones, can together turn outward and touch the world?

Notes

1. Alfred, Lord Tennyson, *Idylls of the King*. The Passing of Arthur, Penguin, London, 418.

Rise Up, Corpse!

It is foolish to expect success if we are merely imitating that which has failed historically. Christians enjoy links with the past, and the continuity of faith and practice is part of the Christian heritage, but does that mean we should always keep on doing things in the same way? There is no future in that survivalist mentality. There are several specific issues I will focus on to illustrate the need for us to be open to change.

The urbanisation following the Industrial Revolution in Great Britain, and the ensuing social upheaval, brought new demands on the life of the churches in the eighteenth and nineteenth centuries. The hours at which they met for services and supporting activities were designed to encourage the good order of a changing society. There was no television and organised entertainment was limited. Sunday evening was a convenient time for people to gather and provided a key opportunity for many evangelistic activities. Many decades later, lots of churches still persist with "the gospel service" or hold to some faded ideal that this is the service best suited to visitors. The social order has changed; many groups have not been successful with this approach. Therefore, why continue?

The JIM Challenge event in Britain, an initiative launched by British Pentecostals during the mid-nineties, "Succeeded in mobilising a very large number of outreach events over eight

weeks, attended by tens of thousands across the country."[1] Some
of the people organising events commented to me how much
easier it was to attract non-Christians to breakfasts at golf clubs,
dinners in restaurants, and many other different events where
the Gospel was clearly presented, rather than to an evangelistic
service in church. More breakfasts and dinners, I say! Those
who have reached the stage where the price of the restaurant
is of less importance than the calories will need to take care of
their food intake! But let us make sure that the methods
of yesterday do not limit the Good News from reaching the
maximum number of people today.

The sharing of Communion has become little more than a
tradition among many groups of Christians. It has degener-
ated into a repetitive liturgy, whether formal or informal, and
has become limited in its specific usefulness. The mechanics
have become ritualistic. I remember going one Sunday morning
to help a tired and weary church. Many of the people were
highly committed and devoted to God and the work of the
Gospel, but through circumstances had become discouraged.
We sang some songs and were approaching the time of
Communion when I sensed the distinct inner-witness of the
Holy Spirit telling me to keep the time dignified but as relaxed
as possible, which I proceeded to do. I cannot remember
the exact details of how we shared the bread and wine, but I
do remember the joy of the majority, which came as a result
of a different approach. These people had been trapped for
several years by a completely inflexible attitude to the administration of Communion. Again, at a recent conference of
leaders I was honoured as the guest and was invited to lead
Communion before the conference adjourned. "Do things
your usual way," they said; but there are so many legitimate
ways of remembering the Lord's supper! I invited everyone
to take enough bread to eat for themselves and also some to
share with others. At first they were nervous, but after we had
all eaten together a wonderful time of fellowship, ministry,

thanksgiving and remembrance engulfed the service. The Bible says,

> *"Is not the cup of thanksgiving for which we give thanks a participation in the blood of Christ? And is not the bread that we break a participation in the body of Christ? Because there is one loaf, we, who are many, are one body, for we all partake of the one loaf."*
>
> (1 Corinthians 10:16–17)

Everybody gave voluble thanks together and we drank the cup. Many said how refreshed and blessed they were simply because the mechanics of the Communion had been approached with freshness and sensitivity.

When considering the teaching and preaching agenda of a church, it is necessary to ask how relevant the programme is to the spiritual needs and the condition of the congregation. If, after years of teaching, many people are still immature, regularly display carnal attitudes and don't seem to be developing a spiritual desire, maybe – amongst other things – we should examine the way in which the leadership teaches and makes disciples.

I have spoken elsewhere about the way in which we make decisions at every level of church life. Some churches, after years of frustration and often more heat than light in deacons' meetings, bad behaviour in church gatherings and a very tenuous scriptural warrant for their democratic practices, still insist on popular vote as their method of government. Why, oh why, do we continue if it does not work?

The Holy Spirit longs for a people whose lives are based on the Word, who come to everything about life, church and ministry with an openness, and are available to Him in a childlike, but not childish, way. How different all our prayer programmes would be! What excitement would flood our main services, with everyone open to God and available to play their part! A Spirit-inspired variety and an expectancy of the supernatural would release the gifts of the Spirit – all of them. New

Testament Christianity would be the order of the day. It *is* still Pentecost, and Jesus *is* still building His Church. Rise up, those long slumbering parts of the Body of Christ! Wake up, those who are asleep! Press forward, those who already live in the experience of that which my words are expressing, until the world, especially tired, preoccupied, materialistic, Western society in its so-called post-Christian lethargy, is drawn to the magnetic reality of New Testament Christianity, down each street, in every village, town and city, so that somewhere, somehow, everybody will be touched by Jesus in action through us.

The Inevitable Consequence

Part of the maturing process, beyond developing a sense of responsibility, is to discover purpose, a reason for living, something upon which to focus ability and energy. Many of the so-called underclass languish because of a lack of these things. Many better-off young people waste much of their talent and become disillusioned by a different road, partly I think because of weak role-models.

People with purpose (some call it destiny) possess a magnetic vibrancy which is highly contagious and addictive. Surely, if such comments are in any part true, the same positives and negatives will work among bodies of people ranging from the local action group to entire nations. This includes the Church, which, as I have said so many times, is described in the Bible as a body. The questions I must ask then are simple: does the Church have a sense of responsibility? And has it, in our generation, discovered its true purpose? These are the signs of maturity. Paul's letter to the Ephesians promotes the idea of maturity with exciting consequences. Think about some sample language from this inspired man who had a huge awareness and revelation of his purpose in life. He said, *"I no longer live, but Christ lives in me"* (Galatians 2:20), and, *"We are . . . created in Christ Jesus to do good works, which God prepared in advance for us to do"* (Ephesians 2:10).

He expressed his confidence, *"that He who began a good work in you will carry it on to completion"* (Philippians 1:6), and challenged, *"See to it that you complete the work you have received in the Lord"* (Colossians 4:17).

I have taken but one verse from each of four consecutive letters. It would be an awe-inspiring study to follow Paul's teachings about predestination, our part in God's eternal purpose, the wonder of grace, the fascination of inheritance, the hope of eternal life; but we can certainly conclude that it is very much part of God's heart to bring us to maturity and to help us grasp the amazing scope of His plans in which we . . .

> *"Are heirs together with Israel, members together of one body, and sharers together in the promise in Jesus Christ."*   (Ephesians 3:6)

This is purpose, destiny, *raison d'être*, meaning. Peter, writing as an older man with his memory full of amazing pictures, words and events from his years of walking the dusty roads of Galilee and Judea with Christ, could have been euphoric about miracles – he saw enough of them. He even saw Jesus replace a soldier's ear that he, Peter, had chopped off moments before. As for teaching, he had heard all of Christ's great messages and concepts. But what most focused the old man's mind? The realisation that Jesus Christ is God, that when his eyes were dazzled on the Mount of Transfiguration, he was seeing the glory, the true nature and splendour of God.

> *"We were eye witnesses of His majesty. For He received honour and glory from God the Father when the voice came to Him from the Majestic Glory, saying, 'This is my Son, whom I love; with Him I am well pleased.'"*   (2 Peter 1:16–17)

Furthermore, Peter knew that *"His divine power"* (2 Peter 1:3) and Peter's own ability to *"participate in the divine nature"* (2 Peter 1:4) had given his existence meaning and enabled him to live an

effective and productive life (2 Peter 1:8). Charles Wesley, in
the famous carol, "Hark! The Herald Angels Sing", expressed
it thus:

> Hail the heaven-born Prince of Peace,
> Hail the Sun of Righteousness.
> Light and life to all He brings,
> Risen with healing in His wings.
> Mild He lays His glory by,
> Born that man no more may die,
> Born to raise the sons of earth,
> Born to give them second birth.

Truly believed, the statement, *"then you will know the truth,
and the truth will set you free"* (John 8:32), would emancipate
the Church, remove its chains and render it credible in a world
which has largely grown to ignore it. David Mainse, the
founder of *100 Huntley Street*, a Canadian television ministry,
has written,

> There are two "main drains" on the effectiveness of the Church
> . . . First, it begins to humanise the divine. Any organisation or
> individual, for that matter, who becomes possessive and protec-
> tive of his faith, rather than creative and innovative, is in serious
> trouble . . . The second distraction is perhaps the most devastat-
> ing. It seems the Church throughout recent history has had an
> interesting ability to become involved with issues that don't
> have any great relevance or impact on the Kingdom of God.[2]

Often the Church is too preoccupied with Her own internal
issues, losing sight of who She really is and therefore how She
is supposed to live.

I believe that there is a huge stirring around the world among
many distinct groups of Christians as realisation dawns that
the time has again come for the people of God to arise, live

with purpose and take up our God-given responsibility of being salt flavouring every part of society and being light replacing the darkness. Someone once said, "Don't curse the darkness, light a candle." The people of God are rising to be the ambassadors of Christ. This is what our belief demands of us, and is what the people of our world, although largely ignorant of it, need.

Imagine Cathedrals of Christian excellence with the Body of Christ awakened to the power of the purpose of its existence. Imagine Western Christianity throwing off the introspection which characterised it at the end of the twentieth century, and joining the spiritual and sociological miracle as millions of people embrace the Christian Gospel in many parts of the developing world. Then, could we say something inevitable would happen again? The twenty-first century Church is becoming as visible and confident worldwide as the huge stone statements of medieval Christianity were physically in their time, standing at the heart of civilisation and at the main crossroads of society. The power of the Gospel that changed the face of civilisation in its early years, and has from time to time risen to its place of service and greatness, is again making impact across the far reaches of life as we know it in our world today.

> *"From Him the whole body, joined and held together by every support-ing ligament, grows and builds itself up in love, as each part does its work."*   (Ephesians 4:16)

Imagine the Universal Church, its national manifestations, Cathedrals – mother churches established in strength through-out the nations, the family church and every outpost, home cell and family group, all joined, held, supported, growing, building, loving and working together for the glory of God. So be it – and quickly, Lord, please! Paul said he was not ashamed of the Gospel. We won't be, either, when we see its raw energy at work. Where should we begin to look for evidence?

Notes

1. Dixon, P., *Signs of Revival*. Kingsway Publications, Eastbourne, 1994, p. 100.
2. Mainse, D., *100 Huntley Street* newsletter, 1991.

I Am Proud of this Message

18

One afternoon Dorothy and I were on one of those relaxing but demanding visits to another town, the cathedral City of Norwich. We enjoyed some food and I'm sure this trip involved visiting some shops – they usually do! I went to sit in the cathedral and as I did, my thoughts ranged through many of the things I have already expressed. I was trying to imagine the atmosphere of a cathedral city centuries ago, when this building would have been the largest landmark and its dominance would have been more than merely structural. "Lord, what does all this mean today?" I asked. I took some time to thank God for His continuing goodness to me. King David's words are a helpful meditation at such times:

> "Who am I, O Sovereign LORD, and what is my family, that you have brought me this far? And as if this were not enough in your sight, O Sovereign LORD, you have also spoken about the future of the house of your servant. Is this your usual way of dealing with man, O Sovereign LORD?" (2 Samuel 7:18–19)

I walked outside into the afternoon sunshine with my heart on fire with praises to God. Seeing the neatly uniformed children from the Cathedral school, my mind switched to thinking of all the establishments I had seen or heard about that were founded in and drew inspiration from the life of Cathedrals: alms houses for the poor and charitable foundations; great hospitals; schools, and even some of the best universities in the world. "But, Lord," I mused, "these are long established institutions. What about now? How does this apply today?"

Thankfully, the slumbering giant of evangelical Christianity is awakening. Churches are increasingly establishing adoption and fostering programmes, pregnancy crisis units, hostels for the young and for those who have been overcome by life's pressures, prison visiting schemes, family access clinics which facilitate visits to the children of broken and divorced families – a full list would take several pages. These programmes are the hands and feet of Jesus, His heart of compassion, and are the inevitable consequence of building a Cathedral of living stones. People and resources are drawn into its life; a godly, anointed leadership works, trains and disciples itself and everyone else in the orbit of its ministry. They all worship, learn together and pray; and everywhere around them God's love and life explodes outwards, bringing help and hope to the lost sheep of humanity.

Many good ministries exist, but most are under-resourced in money and materials. The world is still full of need and there are abundant opportunities to serve. Sadly, much of the Western Church is living in a comfortable cocoon, spending the bulk of its resources upon its internal programmes, largely unaware of the huge possibilities for all to become actively involved, for the whole body to do its work. The chance is offered to all to see the Gospel do what the Gospel can do. Paul said,

> "I am not ashamed of the Gospel, because it is the power of God for the salvation of everyone who believes." (Romans 1:16)

The Good News of Jesus' love is the best news in the world! I am proud of the Gospel of Jesus Christ. The fair and honest study of any community, family or nation, which has embraced the message of the Gospel in any of its twenty centuries of telling, will reveal an enriched, upgraded, happier and healthier people who are naturally, morally, emotionally and spiritually more whole. In short, redemption brings "lift". The perceived freedoms of modern culture bring bondage, while the Gospel brings true freedom.

Several years ago I found myself in a small conference room at Heathrow airport. Few people attended and to all outward appearances the meeting was far from auspicious. After a few introductions the visiting speaker, an American doctor, opened his heart and his Bible to demonstrate the truth that, far from education being the responsibility of the state, it belonged to the parents and the Church. One of the key scriptures he expounded was,

> "Hear, O Israel: The LORD our God, the LORD is one. Love the LORD your God with all your heart and with all your soul and with all your strength. These commandments that I give you today are to be upon your hearts. Impress them on your children. Talk about them when you sit at home and when you walk along the road, when you lie down and when you get up."   (Deuteronomy 6:4–7)

I am told that in the original Scriptures the whole passage is one sentence, demanding the people's attention and obedience. It is hard to convey to you the impact on my mind and spirit which the meeting produced. I had very mixed emotions, but somehow knew I had stumbled across an important truth. In the years since I have witnessed an amazing array of reactions to the concept of a parent-and-church-based, God-centred education programme: contempt, acceptance, furious anger, enthusiasm, indifference, concern, disbelief; in fact, a rainbow of attitudes.

In the legislation enacted after the Second World War, the principle of *in loco parentis* was maintained as the basis for the British educational system, where the school was to act in place of the parent. How happy are parents, given the current climate, that their children are handed over to a man-centred system – humanism? Many parents today are unaware that the education system is steeped in anti-God philosophy where human values and attitudes prevail. This is a sad development from the foundations laid by Christianity in state education which I wish to honour. Unless education – its curriculum, and the hearts and attitudes of its providers – is taught from a God-perspective, children are being let down and damaged. Lessons become man's interpretation of life, based upon reason rather than faith. Where is God in the teaching of History? Or, how can Science be truly understood without acknowledgement of Creator God?

Regarding those neatly-dressed children I saw from the Cathedral school: some of them made up the choir that sang in many of the formal services; historically others were involved in the various activities of its daily life. That seems a good idea, since it is helping children to be thankful and is teaching them to express praise to God, while instilling some discipline and order into the framework of their lives. "But it's brainwashing! Children should not be conditioned in this way!" I hear the liberals cry. This is exactly my point: the Bible, stating its Judeo-Christian philosophy, insists that children will be better prepared for life by being taught from the foundation of God as Creator and Master of the universe. To reiterate: *"Impress* [these commandments] *on your children"* (Deuteronomy 6:7). Market gardeners protect young tomato plants from harm, frost and adverse conditions, treating them better than many liberals treat young children! What kind of philosophy is this, insisting that children are better for knowing both good and evil, being exposed to poisonous and harmful selfishness under the guise of "developing the whole person"?

History tells us that most of the education systems in the Christianised world had their roots in the Church. In Britain there are still thousands of church schools, although how many are working to their original mandate I do not know. It is time the Evangelical and Charismatic wings of the Church established a new movement in our generation: "Back to Basics" in education. Thankfully, in recent years several dozen new schools have been founded, achieving varying levels of success. Much more needs to happen and many more Christian leaders need a vision of our children being educated in accordance with biblical principles. It is not my business to challenge the excellent work being done by dedicated teachers – both Christian and non-Christian – in the various sectors of education, nor is it my purpose to enter the political debate about choices, but I do wish to encourage Christian parents and Christian leaders to face our responsibility in making sure that whatever education is provided for our children remains in agreement with our Christian principles. In many areas this will mean taking the responsibility for the education of our children much more seriously.

The state and independent sectors of education would benefit from having more Christian Head teachers and staff – let us work towards this goal and at the same time establish more Christian schools. It would not take many years with a definite Christian approach to prepare teenagers who can not only cope with educational basics, but who have had the opportunity to understand that privilege and responsibility walk hand in hand, and who can become capable and creditable adult members of society, whether they became Christians or not. If you regard this concept as being rather fanciful, then consider this extract from an authoritative text on education:

> Noting that cultures have failed because they were incapable of changing their old concepts and ways of thinking, he [the consulting economist, Robert Theobald] suggested that we have to help the young people in our culture learn a new set of values, which will allow them to live in a totally different world. The issue, he said, lies here: how do you change the thinking of a culture with enormous speed? Our response is that you do it

through the school system – which is the only social institution that exists to fulfil this function.[1]

The context of this quote was one of technological change, but the principle which it encompasses can be equally applied to the instilling of godly values.

Thinking and talking like this has a price. It was only after my own change of understanding many years ago, after a long pilgrimage and having cleared many doubts, before, with others of equal passion and persuasion, we began our own King's School in 1986, with its three-point emphasis of parent, church and school working to develop each child to their maximum God-given potential. My daughter Sarah was among the first pupils and she benefited from her three years at the school. The facilities have been limited, resources have sometimes been scarce; furthermore, children are children and teachers are teachers! All the tensions typical to school life may be observed, but godly principles are upheld.

Approximately 170 children are being taught at present. One day we believe we will have thousands of children being educated in schools where the curriculum is based around key biblical principles. For our own school in Nottingham, the first principle is that the highest form of knowledge is to know God. The second is that the study of creation must honour God as Creator and Sustainer of all things through Jesus, the Living Word. Colossians 1:16–17 teaches us that,

> *"By Him all things were created: Things in heaven and on earth, visible and invisible, whether thrones or powers or rulers or authorities; all things were created by Him and for Him. He is before all things and in Him all things hold together."*

The third key principle is that God's priorities for learning are first wisdom, then understanding, with knowledge added. We are delighted that this approach is delivering significantly

above-average results, both academically and in the development of each child as a unique individual. The present
curriculum in schools is based upon a secular, humanistic
system. A truly Christian education must promote the Christian
motive for learning and working hard to achieve our best. We
are stewards of the gifts God has given to us: gifts of wisdom,
understanding, knowledge and creativity. We are stewards of
time and are accountable to Him. We don't work hard just for
self-improvement but because we love God and want to serve
others.

However tough it was, the effort was worthwhile. Whatever
it cost, resources have been well spent. The Cathedrals of living
stones need to reproduce in our day what the cathedrals of old
pioneered in theirs. Remember what Deuteronomy 6:7 says:
"Impress [these commandments] *on your children."*

Education is only one area where Christian activity has been
politicised. Other notable examples are hospitals and health
care, social service provision and the probation service, all of
which, at least in part, have been diverted from their original
philosophy and purpose. The hands and feet of Jesus, the Body
of Christ, the Cathedral of living stones, needs, as part of its
compassion-driven and love-providing agenda, to take the field
again in all these areas. There is a strong argument, supported
by historic precedent and current overseas examples that the
churches could provide a better return for the tax-payers'
pound or dollar in many areas of social concern, whilst
continuing to challenge everyone about their personal
responsibility.

Jesus Himself said, *"The poor you will always have with you"*
(Mark 14:7), but this does not excuse society, especially the
Church, from its responsibility. One of the manifestations of
the Spirit of the Lord is a desire for justice:

> *"I will put my Spirit on Him*
> *and he will bring justice to the nations."*   (Isaiah 42:1)

We must therefore help the poor with honesty but not patron-age, especially those who are part of the household of faith, but including the wider challenge provided by the poor, the weak, the vulnerable and the old in our communities.

Much has been written about the division between the rich and poor of society, but the division still remains. The people of God need to be more visible in seeing the power of the Gospel, providing the fishing net in place of the fish, giving help at the minus end of this terrible spectrum while simultaneously using all available means to influence the rich. At my home church in Nottingham, we have made a start, tackling this challenge on the local, national and international level. Three examples serve to illustrate this: through four "Second Chance" shops around the city, which take their name from the second-hand furniture, clothes and other items they sell, we maintain a Christian presence in inner city areas and can use the shops to provide a springboard for friendship within and service to deprived communities. Part of a nationwide initiative, Christians Against Poverty, came to the Christian Centre in 2007, offering a free debt counselling service to anyone, regardless of belief, who is struggling to manage their finances. Looking overseas, our church is helping to pioneer an international development work in Northern Ghana called the King's Village Project, working loosely with local communities to provide clean water and sanitation, education, health care and micro-enterprise opportunities to some of the most disadvantaged people in West Africa. Currently the project school has around 200 pupils and a new intake of 35 pupils joins every year. The project's Medical Centre provides the only doctor amongst 160,000 people, and was recently extended by the construction of a nutritional centre at which severely malnourished children are treated.

Thankfully, this testimony may be repeated thousands of times over the world, but the need requires it to be repeated thousands more. "So, your church is a missionary church," they say when you show any interest in sending people, plans or provisions outside your own "Jerusalem". Surely every church should be a missionary church! Every Cathedral, every living part of the Body of Christ that understands and in any way lives by the ideas of the Bible must be a giving church, a missions church, because not to give would be to burst. Why does even the word "missions" strike fear into so many and leave most of Western Christianity cold and unimpressed, or at best with some token financial and prayer involvement? Missions is terrifying, but it is also exciting. Jesus said,

> *"This Gospel of the Kingdom will be preached in the whole world* [every people group] . . . *and then the end will come."*
>
> (Matthew 24:14)

Missions is therefore intrinsically involved with eschatology. I have already expressed the view that every church should send its senior leaders into a different cultural context regularly. One of the historic strengths of the British churches has been an abundance of good Bible teachers, and the exploding church growth in many parts of the world needs the support of this gift, used with sensitivity and relevance. Could it be true that in exchange Britain and other parts of Western society would benefit from some of the phenomenal evangelistic anointings available in the worldwide Church?

Oswald Smith, of the People's Church in Toronto, was a pioneering thinker and doer in the work of missions, the taking of the whole Gospel to the whole man in the whole world. He believed that taking younger people into missionary situations would further stimulate a missionary call directly, or increase awareness and enthusiasm to support missions for the rest of their lives. He expressed his feelings for missions thus:

> I have found mission fields worthy of every effort we can make for their evangelisation. The waiting multitudes . . . I can never forget.[2]

In some situations special wisdom is needed, in other parts of the world, great bravery, but many places on earth offer opportunities to serve the cause of Christ in missions. We have never had a greater opportunity to reach the thousands of ethnic groups that make up our world than in this generation. This is a well-documented fact.

Outside the Cathedral door, therefore, a plethora of God-glorifying activities continue: the help of the poor and vulnerable; the education of the young; the care of the sick and dying; and the mission of the Church to the ends of the earth. Another important part of the overseeing work performed by the leaders is that of pastoral care for smaller related churches, be they church plants, groups affiliated by relationship, or even by denominational ties. This work, in what the Anglicans call the Diocese, is very important for the health and wellbeing of all the churches. Without this care, too many leaders are left to fend for themselves, feeling lonely and isolated, and because of their feelings of undervalue they often under-perform. A forum for fellowship, input and affirmation is therefore an important function of the Cathedral's leaders. Synergy and team work will have a greater effect over a wider area when the problem of isolation is removed. Flowing out of developed relationships, the greater wisdom of senior leaders is available to the churches, thus avoiding many of the unnecessary problems that occur through unwise action and poor people-management in so many churches. This wider ministry also offers the best resources of administration and advertising to the whole group, and opens the possibility of bringing to maturity more gifted people, because of the wider opportunities for service and better training of leaders.

In all these matters, not to mention the other areas of ministry untouched by this brief overview, we need a new confidence in our message: it is the power of God to salvation. We can be proud of its impact, both historically and in the present day. Donald A. McGavran strongly makes the point:

Let "suburban church" continue social action but not make the capital mistake of saying, "We can't do any evangelism until we do a lot more social action." "Suburban church", to have the greatest joy in Christian life, should be passing on Christ. It must do more evangelism.[3]

I agree. In all our loving actions and social programmes, this sacred duty must never be forgotten.

Notes

1. Postman, N. and Weingartner, C., *Teaching as a Subversive Activity*. Penguin Books Ltd, Harmondsworth, 1971, p. 199.
2. Smith, Oswald J., quoted by L. Neely, *Fire in His Bones*. Tyndale House Publishers Inc., Wheaton, IL, 1982, p. 183.
3. McGavran, D.A. and Arn, W.C., *How To Grow A Church*. G/L Publications, Glendale, CA, 1973, p. 167.

Inspired for the Task

The spiritual Cathedral is filled with vitality and viability; it is New Testament Christianity walking down your street, radically altering the way your city works. The Holy Spirit is busy orchestrating the work of these kingdom-building communities all around the world. Before I concentrate on the inspiration needed for the task, allow me a word about maintaining our focus, keeping His agenda as our agenda, and keeping the sacred duty, the task, always in view. We must be alert and aware that the Church so often finds its time taken by the wrong agenda. This is a human failing, and is not peculiar to the Church. We so easily become defensive and lose our progressive agenda. The following extract is taken from a classic letter written by the Duke of Wellington to the British war office. It illustrates perfectly the ease with which we can lose our focus.

> Gentlemen: Whilst marching to Portugal to a position which commands the approach to Madrid and the French forces, my officers have been diligently complying with your request which has been sent by HM Ship from London to Lisbon and then by despatch rider to our headquarters. We have enumerated our saddles, bridles, tents, and tent poles, and all manner of sundry items for which His Majesty's Government holds me accountable. I have despatched reports on the character, wit, spleen of

every officer. Each item and every farthing has been accounted for, with two regrettable exceptions for which I beg your indulgence. Unfortunately, the sum of one shilling and nine pence remains unaccounted for in one infantry battalion's petty cash and there has been a hideous confusion as to the number of jars of raspberry jam issued to one cavalry regiment during a sandstorm in Western Spain. This reprehensible carelessness may be related to the pressure of circumstances since we are at war with France, a fact which may come as a bit of a surprise to you gentlemen in Whitehall. This brings me to my present purpose, which is to request elucidation of my instructions from His Majesty's Government, so that I may better understand why I am dragging an army over these barren plains. I construe that perforce it must be one of the alternative duties, as given below. I shall pursue one with the best of my ability but I cannot do both. One, to train an army of uniformed British clerks in Spain for the benefit of the accountants and copy-boys in London, or perchance, to see to it that the forces of Napoleon are driven out of Spain.[1]

We have an enemy to fight, whom Jesus identified as a thief: *"The thief comes only to steal and kill and destroy . . . "* but He declared of Himself, *"I have come that they may have life, and have it to the full"* (John 10:10). Don't become sidetracked, it wastes your energy. Paul used the phrase, *"Press on towards the goal"* (Philippians 3:14). This single-minded understanding is important for success and enthusiasm. Stay focused on your task.

I have drawn great inspiration from my study of the Old Testament's "change agents", these "unreasonable" people who refused to accept the *status quo*, but who, with a vision from God and clear goals, set about impossible tasks. I will confine myself to three: Nehemiah, with his great work and the twin prophets Zechariah and Haggai, so different in personality, but propelled by the same vision to see the glory of the House of God return.

If people like J.F. Kennedy can inspire people with his now famous words, "Ask not what your country can do for you, but what you can do for your country" and George Bernard Shaw can challenge, "You see things as they are and ask, 'Why?' But I dream things that never were, and ask, 'Why not?'"² then surely the people of God, inspired by a word from God, can rise up and change impossible situations.

This was the type of setting that confronted Nehemiah. He had heard from some recent visitors to Jerusalem that the people were " . . . *in great trouble and disgrace*" and that *"the wall of Jerusalem is broken down, and its gates have been burned with fire"* (Nehemiah 1:3). This distressed and concerned him. Having heard, he prayed; when he had prayed, he acted. He was sufficiently concerned to break out of his comfortable world in a foreign king's palace, and commissioned by God he threw himself with commitment into changing the state of the city of his fathers. Many good principles unfold to us as, in the face of strong opposition, he succeeds in his task. I will mention a few:

1. **He went with the king's blessing** (Nehemiah 2:8–9). He realised the need to go with authority.
2. **He went with a specific purpose.** *"So that I can rebuild* [the city]" (Nehemiah 2:5). Much has been taught in many places about goal setting. The truth is, if you aim for the moon you may well succeed in hitting it. You will almost certainly reach further than you would have done without the goal.
3. **He had a clear timetable.** *"So I set a time"* (Nehemiah 2:6).
4. **He identified himself with the problem.** *"I confess the sins we Israelites, including myself and my fathers house have committed against you"* (Nehemiah 1:6).
5. **He appraised himself of the situation and counted the cost.** *"I set out during the night, through the valley gate . . . "* (Nehemiah 2:11–15). Jesus Himself advised on the wisdom of counting the cost (see Luke 14:28–30).

6. **He did not speak too soon**. *"As yet I had said nothing"* (Nehemiah 2:16).
7. **He challenged the people**. *"Let us rebuild the walls"* (Nehemiah 2:17). Using God's past blessing and evidence of His gracious hand he urged them to rebuild and remove their disgrace.

And all of this took place before the real work had even begun! We can see from this that care in planning and preparation are a vital part of the success of any worthwhile project. Nehemiah had a vision which helped his planning, but he had to continually resist those who tried to thwart his progress. I regard them as vandals on Nehemiah's building site. Every worthwhile project will be opposed and Nehemiah found his enemies within and without. When they heard of his building project they were very much disturbed (Nehemiah 2:10) and resorted initially to mockery and ridicule of the Jews (Nehemiah 2:19 and Nehemiah 4:1). As the project proceeded this developed into anger (Nehemiah 4:7), which eventually gave birth to scheming (Nehemiah 6:2), lying and blackmail (Nehemiah 6:6), and proceeded into false prophecy (Nehemiah 6:12) and intimidation (Nehemiah 6:13).

In the face of all the enemies, Nehemiah told his people,

> *"Don't be afraid of them. Remember the LORD, who is great and awesome, and fight for your brothers, your sons and your daughters, your wives and your homes."*   (Nehemiah 4:14)

After speaking this encouragement, the people worked and worked and worked. The man who had the trumpet stayed with Nehemiah; I suppose the prophet and the apostle build well together! There was more trouble, scheming and messengers, and then comes his unforgettable reply to his opponents:

> *"I am carrying on a great project and cannot go down."*
>   (Nehemiah 6:3)

As a consequence of Nehemiah's persistence,

> *"The wall was completed* [and] . . . *all the surrounding nations were afraid and lost their self-confidence, because they realised that this work had been done with the help of God."*
>
> (Nehemiah 6:14–16)

Whatever your vision, however bad the opposition, may faith and inspiration awaken in you that it is God's work, and through you He intends to finish what He has begun.

The twin prophecies of Haggai and Zechariah, written about the same period of restoration in Old Testament history, further inspire me to believe for enormous change in what may appear to be impossible situations. Zechariah was asked one of the Bible's great questions: *"What do you see?"* (Zechariah 4:2). Part of his answer revealed a wisdom we all need; we don't have all the answers. The Lord's words, *"not by my might nor by power, but by my Spirit"* (Zechariah 4:6), must never be forgotten. The mountains, the insurmountable difficulties, will become level ground, and all of us are reminded not to despise the day of small things. That is but a sample of chapter 4; the language flows with grandeur, since Zechariah is a visionary. In that capacity, he played his part in the rebuilding of the temple too.

Haggai is much more straight-hitting and plain-speaking. The four prophecies, delivered over three-and-a-half months and condensed into two chapters, stimulated a dramatic change in attitude and behaviour after the years in which the temple had been neglected and provoked continuing action until the job was finished.

What can we learn from these prophets? It is initially obvious that the Word of the Lord has the power to change any situation. More specifically, I believe they offer both a challenge and a hope to the Church in many countries. I have deepest concern for my own country, but my travels have allowed me to observe that the message applies in many places. I am also sure that many other people would benefit from hearing the voice of the Holy Spirit in these prophesies. Furthermore, the principles will work outside the often-closed world of church life.

First, Haggai seeks for an honest review. He insists that the people of God have been careless and unsuccessful, telling them that they had:

1. **Believed a lie** (Haggai 1:2)
2. **Adopted wrong priorities** (Haggai 1:4)
3. **Poor results** (Haggai 1:5,6,9)
4. **Concern only for their own affairs** (Haggai 1:9; 2:16–17)
5. **Been historically disobedient** (Haggai 1:12)

In spite of this dreadful catalogue of failure, God, through the prophet, assures the people, *"I am with you"* (Haggai 1:13). The prophetic flow stirs the people with a vision to be captured as the Lord "stirs up the spirit" of the leaders. Then comes a call to purity. The people are informed of their defiled condition (Haggai 2:14), but are affirmed as being different with the staggering, *"I will bless you"* (Haggai 2:19). Earlier in chapter 2 came a continuing and comforting promise that, though the people had been shaken, they must again be strong (Haggai 2:4), because God will fill the rebuilt house with His promised glory.

In spite of their selfish state when the prophet began speaking, God assures them, *"I am with you."* How gracious and compassionate is the Lord's love.

The questions come through the centuries to us. Have we been careless? Are we as successful as we should be? Do we see the vision of God's purpose in our lives as clearly as we could? Are we a holy people? Do we really believe that God is committed to a glorious Church? So many questions, I know, but we must face the facts that while we are thrilled with all the Lord has done, we of the Western Church are not in the vanguard of the move of the Spirit to the extent that we should be.

"Be not afraid of greatness! Some are born great, some achieve greatness, and some have greatness thrust upon them."[3]

God's commitment is to a Spirit-filled bride, a building in which He lives, a Body which is the fullness of Christ. If this is true, we have an obligation to greatness. Greatness is being what He wants us to be, knowing what He wants us to know and doing what He wants us to do. This inspires me to stay the distance and finish the race. I am personally inspired to see a Cathedral of living stones built. Collectively, we have made a start. What are you inspired to accomplish?

Notes

1. Quoted by David Hamilton-Williams in *Waterloo: New Perspectives. The Great Battle Reappraised*. Arms and Armour Press, London, 1993, p. 129.
2. Shaw, G.B., quoted by J. Stott, *Issues Facing Christians Today*, (1st ed.). Marshall, Morgan and Scott, Basingstoke, 1984, p. 329.
3. Shakespeare, W., *Twelfth Night*, II, iv, 158.

Epilogue

I trust that something of my passion and love for God have come through the words of this book, urging you forward to live for the glory of God. At the end of the second chapter we considered several truths. Now it's time to test the strength of our convictions. I have at times used the following checklist to challenge me in my spiritual walk. Personally, I find it both helpful and sobering. I trust that you will too.

1. Was I ever further forward spiritually than I am now?
2. Am I prepared to change?
3. Is my reading of the Bible a duty or a delight?
4. Am I deeply conscious of the need for more prayer, privately and corporately?
5. Do I live day by day in conscious dependence upon the Lord?
6. Have I wounded or hurt anyone and not yet apologised?
7. How long is it since I last shed tears over the condition of the world and the Church?
8. Am I fighting a losing battle with evil thoughts?
9. When did I last undertake a spiritual fast?
10. Am I a faithful steward of all the money that I receive?

If the building of God's house in you personally is not developing in the way the Master Architect and Builder planned it, please change now. Become a pilgrim with me so that each of us, as living stones, will be built together to make a house fit for the glory of God.

About the author

David Shearman is the Senior Minister of the Christian Centre, Nottingham, a position he has held since 1977.

As well as being committed to the church and the city of Nottingham, David maintains a busy schedule of preaching all over the world. David operates with a very strong apostolic and prophetic anointing that sharpens, shapes and impacts leaders around the world. He is also the author of several books.

David is married to Dorothy and they have two grown up children (themselves married) and four grandchildren.

We hope you enjoyed reading this New Wine book.
For details of other New Wine books
and a wide range of titles from other
Word and Spirit publishers visit our website:
www.newwineministries.co.uk
email: newwine@xalt.co.uk